READING GROUP CHOICES 2010

Selections for lively book discussions

Published in the United States by **Reading Group Choices**,
a division of Connxsys LLC
ISBN: 978-0-9759742-5-4

For further information, contact:
Barbara Drummond Mead
Reading Group Choices
532 Cross Creek Court
Chester, MD 21619
Toll-free: 1-866-643-6883
info@ReadingGroupChoices.com
www.ReadingGroupChoices.com

welcome to
READING GROUP *Choices*

Reading Group Choices is so proud to be a "pioneer" in providing resources for reading groups. But even as we reflect on our 16th annual edition of *Reading Group Choices: Selections for Lively Book Discussions*, we are struck by the longevity of some of the groups we support and by their remarkable diversity. We have heard of one group this year that has been in operation for over 75 years, its founders passing on their excitement and membership to those in the next generation! And we hear of reading groups helping homeless, mentally ill, and imprisoned members to step away from their troubles for a bit and to build friendships and confidence at the same time.

Readers everywhere enjoy the pleasure, adventure, knowledge, self aware-ness, and solace that come between the covers of a book. Members of reading groups want to share their enjoyment with friends and colleagues. If the rapid growth of subscribers to *Reading Group Choices* online and print publications is any indication, the popularity of book groups among a wide range of age groups, geography, and background is gaining prevalence. People are gathering to share the joy of reading in their homes, in coffee shops, in libraries, in theaters, in bookstores, in parks— just about anywhere conducive to lively discussion.

The titles found in *Reading Group Choices 2010* have been selected for their heart-felt, humorous, memorable, controversial, and insightful ideas —frequently fictional and occasionally factual—from authors both well-known and emerging.

We are grateful to our readers and to our partners in the publishing and bookselling fields for the steady stream of suggestions and welcome encouragement they have provided. We look forward to continuing to support you and your colleagues in the thrill of shared reading. Here's to another year of friendship and discussion!

And, thanks for keeping the joy of reading alive.

—BARBARA AND CHARLIE MEAD

Book Group Favorites

Early in 2009, we asked thousands of book groups to tell us what books they read and discussed during the previous year that they enjoyed most. The top ten titles were:

1. **Water for Elephants** *by Sara Gruen* (Algonquin)

2. **Loving Frank** *by Nancy Horan* (Ballantine Books)

3. **Three Cups of Tea** *by Greg Mortenson and David Oliver Relin* (Penguin Books)

4. **The Glass Castle** *by Jeannette Walls* (Scribner)

5. **A Thousand Splendid Suns** *by Khaled Hosseini* (Riverhead Trade)

6. **The Book Thief** *by Marcus Zusak* (Knopf Books for Young Readers)

7. **Eat, Pray, Love** *by Elizabeth Gilbert* (Penguin Books)

8. **The Shack** *by William P. Young* (Windblown Media)

9. **Snow Flower and the Secret Fan** *by Lisa See* (Random House Trade)

10. **The Guernsey Literary and Potato Peel Pie Society** *by Mary Ann Shaffer and Annie Barrows* (The Dial Press)

Contents

GUIDELINES FOR
Lively Book Discussions

Respect space—Avoid "crosstalk" or talking over others.

Allow space—Some of us are more outgoing and others more reserved. If you've had a chance to talk, allow others time to offer their thoughts as well.

Be open—Keep an open mind, learn from others, and acknowledge there are differences in opinion. That's what makes it interesting!

Offer new thoughts—Try not to repeat what others have said, but offer a new perspective.

Stay on the topic—Contribute to the flow of conversation by holding your comments to the topic of the book, keeping any personal references to an appropriate minimum.

CONVERSATION STARTERS
General ideas to stimulate your book group discussion.

Discuss factual questions and recap the story:

- Who are the key characters?

- Does one or more characters tell the story? How does this affect the narrative?

- Are they believable characters?

- How do their experiences cause them to grow?

- What are the themes?

- What are the conflicts in the story?

- How does the setting and time period affect the story?

Discuss how the story relates to your life:

- How would you react to the same situations?

- Have any of the events in the story happened in your life?

- If a historical story, what would be the advantages/ disadvantages of living in that period? Would you like it? Why? What if it's a science fiction story?

- Look at the jacket. Is it one you would have chosen for this book? Why or why not?

- Did the story change your opinion of a place, event, time period, etc.? How so?

- What do you think will happen to the characters next?

- If the story is made into a movie, whom would you pick to play the characters?

29 GIFTS
How a Month of Giving Can Change Your Life

AUTHOR: *Cami Walker*

PUBLISHER: Da Capo Lifelong Books, October 2009

WEBSITE: www.29giftsbook.com

AVAILABLE IN:
Hardcover, 256 pages, $19.95
ISBN: 978-0-7382-1356-9

SUBJECT: Inspiration/Personal Challenges/ Self-Help (Nonfiction)

SUMMARY: One month after her wedding day, thirty-three-year-old Cami Walker was diagnosed with multiple sclerosis, and the life she knew changed forever. Cami was soon in and out of LA's emergency rooms with alarming frequency as she battled the neurological condition that left her barely able to walk and put enormous stress on her marriage. Each day brought new negative thoughts: *I'm going to end up in a wheelchair. Mark's probably going to leave me. My life is over. Why did this have to happen to me?*

Then, as a remedy for her condition, Cami received an uncommon prescription from a friend, an African medicine woman named Mbali Creazzo; Give away 29 gifts in 29 days.

The gifts, Mbali said, could be anything, but their giving had to be both authentic and mindful. At least one gift needed to be something she felt was scarce in her life.

29 Gifts is Cami's poignant and unforgettable story of embracing the natural process of giving and receiving. By Day 29, not only had her health and happiness turned around, but she had also embarked on creating a worldwide giving movement.

29 Gifts shows how a simple, daily practice of altruism can dramatically alter your outlook on the world.

ABOUT THE AUTHOR: **Cami Walker** lives in Hollywood, California, with her husband, Mark.

1. What is your first impression of Cami when we meet her in the pro-logue? Does it change by the end of the book, and if so, how?

2. Do you think that Mbali's admonition to Cami to "stop thinking about yourself" is fair, considering Cami's condition?

3. Is Mbali's suggestion to lift Cami out of her "black hole" by giving away 29 gifts in 29 days one that you think would work in your own life if you were confronted with similar circumstances?

4. Is there someone in your life like Dr. Kim who has changed your per-ception of the world and your place in it? In what ways?

5. Mbali tells Cami, "When you are overgiving, you are not living in abundance, but in scarcity. . . . When you give from a place of service, honesty, and fullness, you are left feeling revitalized." Do you agree with Mbali, and if so, why?

6. What role does meditation play in Cami's life, and in what ways does it help her address feelings of distress in her life?

7. Cami writes, "One of the profound changes I've seen for myself since I began giving is that I now feel comfortable counting every gift I mindfully offer to another person. I no longer feel pressure to make a grand gesture for it to count." Do you feel you're always mindful of your intention in giving someone a gift?

8. Of all the gifts that Cami gives in her first 29 days, is there one that resonates more for you than another? Which one and why?

9. Is there a story from the *29 Gifts* community at the conclusion of the book that touches you more than another?

10. If you were to start the *29 Gifts* program today, who would be the first person on your list to receive a gift, and why? What would you like to give that person?

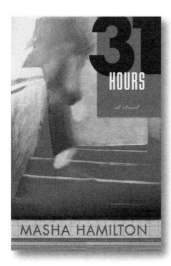

31 HOURS

AUTHOR: *Masha Hamilton*

PUBLISHER: Unbridled Books, 2009

WEBSITE: www.unbridledbooks.com
www.mashahamilton.com

AVAILABLE IN:
Hardcover, 329 pages, $24.95
ISBN: 978-1-932961-83-6

SUBJECT: Family/Spirituality/
Culture & World Issues (Fiction)

"Equal parts thriller and poetry, Masha Hamilton's 31 Hours *had me turning pages late into the night."*—**Meg Waite Clayton, author of the novel** *The Wednesday Sisters*

SUMMARY: A woman in New York awakens knowing, as deeply as a mother's blood can know, that her grown son is in danger. She has not heard from him in weeks. His name is Jonas. His girlfriend, Vic, doesn't know what she has done wrong, but Jonas won't answer his cell phone. We soon learn that Jonas is isolated in a safe-house apartment in New York City, pondering his conversion to Islam and his experiences training in Pakistan, preparing for the violent action he has been instructed to take in 31 hours. Carried by Hamilton's highly-lauded prose, this story about the helplessness of those who cannot contact a beloved young man who is on a devastatingly confused path is compelling on the most human level. In our world, when a family loses track of an idealistic son, an entire city could be in danger.

ABOUT THE AUTHOR: **Masha Hamilton** is the author of three previous novels, *Staircase of a Thousand Steps* (2001), *The Distance Between Us* (2004), and *The Camel Bookmobile* (2007). As a journalist, she has covered Africa, Russia, the Middle East, and most recently Afghanistan. She is a licensed shiatsu practitioner and is currently studying nuad phaen boran, Thai traditional massage. She lives with her family in Brooklyn.

1. Carol struggles with how involved she can get as a mother when she's worried about her young adult son. How *does* parenting change as children become young adults? Do you think she does too much, too little, or enough?

2. What factors contribute to Jonas finding himself in the circumstances that he does as the novel begins? Is it possible to feel sympathetic toward him?

3. The New York City Subway is a force in the novel. How do different characters perceive the subway?

4. The diverse meaning of prayer is one of the novel's themes. Sonny Hurt, the subway panhandler, views the subway as a holy place, a kind of church. And both Jonas and Mara try to pray in unusual ways. What role does prayer plan in tying together Jonas and the other characters?

5. Jonas and Masoud both have somewhat distant relationships with their fathers. How might this have impacted their character development and the story's outcome?

6. What would have happened if Jonas had been able to reach Vic by cell phone sometime during those 31 hours?

7. What do you think will happen to the relationship between Carol and Jake after the novel ends?

8. In the final chapters, Jonas leaves nails behind. What is the significance of that act?

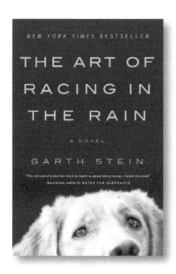

THE ART OF RACING IN THE RAIN

AUTHOR: **Garth Stein**

PUBLISHER: Harper paperbacks, 2009

WEBSITE: www.harpercollins.com
www.GoEnzo.com

AVAILABLE IN:
Trade Paperback, 336 pages, $14.99
ISBN: 978-0-06-153796-7

SUBJECT: Animals/Relationships/Family
(Fiction)

*"Moving. . . . [Readers will] delight in Enzo's wild, original voice; his aching insights into the limitations and joys of the canine and human worlds; and his infinite capacity for love. A natural choice for book clubs."—**Booklist***

SUMMARY: Enzo knows he is different from other dogs: a philosopher with a nearly human soul, he has educated himself by watching television and by listening very closely to the words of his master, Denny Swift, an up-and-coming race car driver. On the eve of his death, Enzo takes stock of his life, recalling all that he and his family have been through: the sacrifices Denny has made to succeed professionally; the unexpected loss of Eve, Denny's wife; the three-year battle over their daughter, Zoë, whose maternal grandparents pulled every string to gain custody. In the end, despite what he sees as his own limitations, Enzo comes through heroically to preserve the Swift family, holding in his heart the dream that Denny will become a racing champion with Zoë at his side. Having learned what it takes to be a compassionate and successful person, the wise canine can barely wait until his next lifetime, when he is sure he will return as a man.

ABOUT THE AUTHOR: **Garth Stein**, the author of two novels—*How Evan Broke His Head and Other Secrets* and *Raven Stole the Moon,* and a play, *Brother Jones*—has also worked as a documentary filmmaker.

1. Some early readers of the novel have observed that viewing the world through a dog's eyes makes for a greater appreciation of being human. Why do you think this is?

2. Enzo's observations throughout the novel provide insight into his world view. For example: *"The visible becomes inevitable."* *"Understanding the truth is simple. Allowing oneself to experience it, is often terrifically difficult."* *"No race has ever been won in the first corner; many races have been lost there."* How does his philosophy apply to real life?

3. In one of the book's darkest moments, one of Zoe's stuffed animals—the zebra—comes to life and torments Enzo. What does the zebra symbolize?

4. Can you imagine the novel being told from Denny's point of view? How would it make the story different?

5. In the first chapter, Enzo says: *"It's what's inside that's important. The soul. And my soul is very human."* How does Enzo's situation—a human soul trapped in a dog's body—influence his opinions about what he sees around him? How do you feel about the ideas of reincarnation and karma as Enzo defines them?

6. Do you find yourself looking at your own dog differently after reading this novel?

7. In the book, we get glimpses into the mindset and mentality of a race car driver. What parallels can you think of between the art of racing and the art of living?

8. The character of Ayrton Senna, as he is presented in the book, is heroic, almost a mythic figure. Why do you think this character resonates so strongly for Denny?

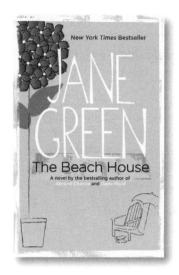

THE BEACH HOUSE

AUTHOR: *Jane Green*

PUBLISHER: Plume Books, 2009

WEBSITE: www.penguingroup.com
www.janegreen.com

AVAILABLE IN:
Trade Paperback, 352 pages, $15.00
ISBN: 978-0-452-29538-4

SUBJECT: Family/Relationships/
Women's Lives (Fiction)

"Green gives you a clear sense of Nantucket's weathered splendor and offers up a refreshing summertime getaway...best read on a deck chair somewhere."—**Chicago Sun-Times**

SUMMARY: Nan Powell is a free-spirited, sixty-five-year-old widow who's not above skinny-dipping in her neighbors' pools when they're away and who dearly loves her Nantucket home. But when she discovers that the money she thought would last forever is dwindling, she realizes she must make drastic changes to save her beloved house. So Nan takes out an ad: *Rooms to rent for the summer in a beautiful old Nantucket home with water views and direct access to the beach.*

Slowly people start moving in to the house, filling it with noise, laughter, and with tears. As the house comes alive again, Nan finds her family and friends expanding. Her son comes home for the summer, and then an unexpected visitor turns all their lives upside down. As she did so masterfully in her *New York Times* bestseller *Second Chance*, Jane Green once again proves herself one of the preeminent writers of contemporary women's fiction.

ABOUT THE AUTHOR: **Jane Green** is the internationally bestselling author of *The Other Woman, Swapping Lives*, and *Second Chance*. Before achieving great success with her first novel, *Straight Talking*, Green worked as a journalist in the United Kingdom. A mother of four, she currently resides in Connecticut with her partner and children. This is her tenth novel.

1. Nan finds a certain freedom in her old age that most women don't even have in their youth. In what ways can old age be liberating for a woman? Do you know anyone like Nan? Do you hope to be like Nan?

2. For Nan, family extends beyond blood relations, from Sarah to the summer guests. Who in your own life do you recognize as family even if you're not related? How and why do these relationships develop? Which relationships are stronger—those we have by birth or those we make during the course of our lives?

3. Choose the two characters you found the most compelling and map out their respective journeys through the course of the novel. What were the turning points in their stories? Why did you find these characters the most affecting?

4. Daff is conflicted by her love for her daughter and her enjoyment in their spending time apart from each other, and the same feeling, although not as delicately articulated, is clearly true for Jess as well. What is your opinion of Daff as a mother? Have you ever wanted to get away from your own family?

5. Identify each character's major flaw as well as his or her most redeeming quality. What examples from the book best illustrate these traits?

6. Discuss the struggle each character experiences with fidelity; remember that fidelity is not only a romantic concern. What does it mean to be faithful? What are the differences (and, sometimes, conflicts) between being faithful to one's self and to another person?

7. Both Daff and Daniel are returning to the singles scene after being married for many years, although they do so for different reasons. Contrast Daniel's and Daff's first attempts at romance. Does either of their experiences connect with your own?

8. Location can have great emotional significance, bringing us back to a memory or helping us become someone new. What does Windermere represent for each of the characters? Is there a place in the world that is meaningful for you in the same way?

9. Imagine you are writing another chapter of *The Beach House* that takes place five years after the novel ends. What would you include? What more would you like to know about these characters?

10. If you could ask Jane Green one question, what would it be?

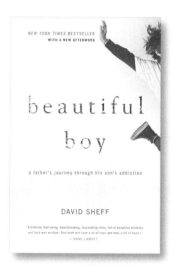

BEAUTIFUL BOY
A Father's Journey Through His Son's Addiction

AUTHOR: *David Sheff*

PUBLISHER: Mariner Books, 2009

WEBSITE: www.hmhbooks.com
www.davidsheff.com

AVAILABLE IN:
Trade Paperback, 352 pages, $14.95
ISBN: 978-0-547-20388-1

SUBJECT: Biography/Family/
Personal Challenges (Memoir)

"This is a brilliant, harrowing, heart-breaking, fascinating book, full of beautiful moments and hard-fought wisdom. This book is going to save a lot of lives, and help heal a lot of hearts. I absolutely could not put it down: I read it straight through in two nights."—**Anne Lamott, author of** *Grace (Eventually), Bird by Bird,* **and** *Operating Instructions*

SUMMARY: What had happened to my beautiful boy? To our family? What did I do wrong? Those are the wrenching questions that haunted every moment of David Sheff's journey through his son Nic's addiction to drugs and tentative steps toward recovery. Before Nic Sheff became addicted to crystal meth, he was a charming boy, joyous and funny, a varsity athlete and honor student adored by his two younger siblings. After meth, he was a trembling wraith who lied, stole, and lived on the streets. David Sheff traces the first subtle warning signs: the denial, the 3 A.M. phone calls (is it Nic? the police? the hospital?), the rehabs. His preoccupation with Nic became an addiction in itself, and the obsessive worry and stress took a tremendous toll. But as a journalist, he instinctively researched every avenue of treatment that might save his son and refused to give up on Nic.

ABOUT THE AUTHOR: **David Sheff** books include *Game Over, China Dawn,* and *All We Are Saying.* Sheff and his family live in Inverness, California.

1. Why are addiction memoirs so addictive? Why were you drawn to this one?
2. David Sheff writes that "drug stories are sinister." What does he mean by that? How are drug stories different than addiction memoirs, if at all?
3. Which of Sheff's experiences, thoughts, and actions were most affecting to you? Which could you relate to and which were totally foreign?
4. Sheff begins his story with the statement, "We are among the first generation of self-conscious parents. Before us, people had kids. We parent." What does it mean to parent, as opposed to just having kids? What does Sheff learn about "parenting" over the course of the book?
5. Did you view Sheff as a "good parent"?
6. What is the extent of David Sheff's own drug use? Would you be—or have you been—honest about your past with your own kids?
7. Discuss Nic's descent. When do you think you would have noticed Nic had a serious problem and needed help? Did you disagree with David Sheff's course of action? What might you have done differently?
8. When David smoked pot with Nic, what was your reaction?
9. A friend of David's expresses surprise at Nic's addiction and says the Sheffs don't seem like a dysfunctional family. Sheff responds, "We are dysfunctional. . . . I'm not sure I know any 'functional' families." How would you define a functional family? Which are the Sheffs? How you would describe your own family?
10. Many of the counselors and family members of addicts tell David and Karen, "Be allies. Remember, take care of yourselves. You'll be good for no one—for each other, for your children—if you don't." Do Karen and David take care of one another? Does David take care of himself?
11. What toll does Nic's addiction take on Jasper and Daisy? How do David and Karen help them to understand their brother's behavior?
12. At the end of his memoir, Sheff writes, "Now I am in my own program to recover from my addiction to [Nic's addiction]." How is Sheff addicted to Nic's addiction? How does David's addiction affect his family, his job, and his life? What is his program for recovery?
13. Nic Sheff's own memoir, *Tweak*, was published simultaneously with *Beautiful Boy*. Having only read the latter, would it surprise you to learn that Nic, during the height of his drug abuse, dealt drugs? That he prostituted himself for drug money? As a parent, do you think it would be worse knowing or not knowing such details?
14. When the book ends, Nic is once again in recovery. Are you left hopeful he will stay that way?

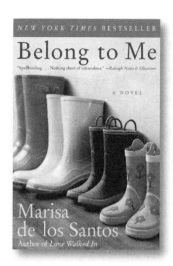

BELONG TO ME

AUTHOR: *Marisa de los Santos*

PUBLISHER: Harper paperbacks, 2009

Website: www.marisadelossantos.com
www.harpercollins.com

AVAILABLE IN:
Trade Paperback, 416 pages, $13.99
ISBN: 978-0-061-24028-7

SUBJECT: Family/Relationships/
Women's Lives (Fiction)

"The novel reveals layers of rich patina—the story underneath is more complex, engaging, and surprisingly moving . . . de los Santos delivers an interconnected network of compelling little stories. Her writing is both vividly descriptive and surprisingly insightful."—The Boston Globe

SUMMARY: Cornelia Brown surprised herself when she was gripped by the sudden, inescapable desire to move to the suburbs with her husband. Her mettle is quickly tested by her impeccably dressed, overly judgmental neighbor Piper Truitt—the embodiment of everything Cornelia feared she'd find in suburbia. With Lake, another recent arrival, Cornelia shares a love of literature and old movies—as she forms an instant bond with this warm yet elusive woman and her perceptive, brilliant young son Dev.

Acclaimed bestselling author Marisa de los Santos's literary talents shine in the complex interactions she creates between three unforgettable women, deftly entangling her characters in a web of trust, betrayal, love, and loss that challenges them in ways they never imagined.

ABOUT THE AUTHOR: An award-winning poet and bestselling author with a Ph.D. in literature and creative writing, **Marisa de los Santos** lives in Wilmington, Delaware, with her husband and children. She's the author of the bestseller *Love Walked In*.

1. Each character faces a different challenge: what are these challenges and how do they handle them? Who has changed the most by the end of the novel?

2. When we meet Cornelia's neighbor, Piper, she is commenting on Cornelia's lawn and home, suggesting changes. Does she have a right to criticize Piper's lawn and home? How did this make you feel? What does it mean to be a good neighbor?

3. Piper confesses that she finds security through organizing, but when her best friend, Elizabeth becomes ill, this surprise rattles her carefully organized world. What does safety mean? What rituals, if any, do you have to create a feeling of safety?

4. What is Dev's relationship with his mother like? Do you think mothers and sons have a different relationship than mothers and daughters or fathers and sons? Why or why not? What do Dev and Lake learn from each other?

5. Part of the way into the story Dev embarks on a quest to find his father? What issues does he face? If you were Dev would you look for your father? Why or why not?

6. Near the end of the novel Lake says that everything she's done has been for Dev. Is this acceptable? Is it ok to lie to protect the people you love?

7. Do you think Clare's and Dev's relationship is an accurate depiction of first love? How does their relationship differ from the other romantic relationships in the novel? What do you think will happen between them in the future?

8. How would you describe Cornelia's childbirth experience? How does it lead her to make a decision that would change the lives of the people in her life?

9. What does "family" mean and how is this explored in the novel? Is it possible for one person to belong to another?

10. Cornelia compares life to the movies. What if any movie does the novel remind you of? Is there a movie(s) that you could compare to your life?

BETWEEN THE ASSASSINATIONS

AUTHOR: *Aravind Adiga*

PUBLISHER: Free Press, 2009

WEBSITE: www.simonandschuster.com
www.aravindadiga.com

AVAILABLE IN:
Hardcover, 352 pages, $24.00
ISBN: 978-1-439-15292-8

SUBJECT: Relationships/Culture &
World Issues/Social Issues (Fiction)

"Between the Assassinations *shows that Adiga . . . is one of the most important voices to emerge from India in recent years."—**The Guardian** **(London)**

SUMMARY: Welcome to Kittur, India. It's on India's southwestern coast, bounded by the Arabian Sea to the west and the Kaliamma River to the south and east. And if the characters in *Between the Assassinations* are any indication, Kittur is an extraordinary crossroads of the brightest minds and the poorest morals, the up-and-coming and the downtrodden, and the poets and the prophets of an India that modern literature has rarely addressed.

Between the Assassinations showcases the most beloved aspects of Adiga's writing to brilliant effect: the class struggle rendered personal; the fury of the underdog and the fire of the iconoclast; and the prodigiously ambitious narrative talent. A blinding, brilliant, and brave mosaic of Indian life as it is lived in a place called Kittur, *Between the Assassinations*, with all the humor, sympathy, and unflinching candor of *The White Tiger*, enlarges our understanding of the world we live in today.

ABOUT THE AUTHOR: **Aravind Adiga** was born in India in 1974 and attended Columbia and Oxford universities. A former correspondent for *Time* magazine, he has also been published in the *Financial Times*. He lives in Mumbai, India.

1. The symbols of each major religion act "like signposts to identify the three religions of the town to voyagers from the ocean (p.39)." Do you think these symbols act as a warning to visitors or are they welcoming signs of the diversity of Kittur? Discuss the relationships these three world religions have with each other within the city and the tensions they cause among its inhabitants.

2. In what ways do the characters in the book struggle with the issues of caste and class in Indian society? How do characters use caste and class to define themselves and their relationships with others?

3. Discuss how the travel guide descriptions of Kittur embellish and contribute to the development of the city's character, as well as to the individual characters in each of the stories. How do the descriptions act as a foil to the very personal, individual vignettes and unite them into a whole?

4. The assistant headmaster D'Mello is disillusioned with the state of the Indian government, and yet there are hints in the story of his past idealism that are revealed when he speaks to or thinks of his student, Girish. What do you suppose happened to D'Mello and how might Girish remind him of his past? Discuss why he feels compelled to share secrets with the young boy—is he trying to protect his idealism of youth? Live vicariously through the boy? Or protect him from the very idealism that turned against D'Mello?

5. While Ratna is waiting in a bus station with the diseased boy who was going to marry his daughter, a stranger says to them, "We'll have to hand this country back to the British or the Russians or someone, I tell you. We're not meant to be masters of our own fate" (p. 287). How is this underlying thought represented in the stories throughout the book? How does it permeate the minds of many of the characters? Discuss the circumstances in Kittur that may have led to these attitudes.

6. Truth is preserved in gossip and rumor more so than in the newspapers in Kittur. Corruption runs rampant through the police and the government. How do the characters subtly fight this? What is holding them back from doing more?

7. Discuss Indian Communism and its interpretation of caste. In what ways does it become its own kind of caste and why do you think it is seen as one to be avoided?

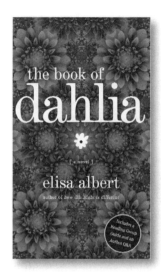

THE BOOK OF DAHLIA

AUTHOR: *Elisa Albert*

PUBLISHER: Free Press, 2009

WEBSITE: www.simonandschuster.com
         www.elisaalbert.com

AVAILABLE IN:
Trade Paperback, 288 pages, $14.00
ISBN: 978-0-743-29130-9

SUBJECT: Family/Relationships/
Personal Challenges (Fiction)

"Albert creates a heroine who is as hilarious as she is honest, and she does it without a shred of sentimentality."—**People** magazine

"Albert writes with the black humor of Lorrie Moore and a pathos that is uniquely her own, all the more blistering for being slyly invoked."
—**The New Yorker**

SUMMARY: Meet Dahlia Finger: twenty-nine, depressed, whip-smart, occasionally affable, bracingly honest, resolutely single, and perennially unemployed. She spends her days stoned in front of the TV, watching the same movies repeatedly, like "a form of prayer." But when Dahlia's so-called life is upended by a terminal brain tumor, she must work toward reluctant emotional reckoning with the aid of a questionable self-help guide. With her take-no-prisoners perspective, her depressive humor, and her extreme vulnerability, Dahlia Finger walks a dazzling line between gravitas and irreverence, compassion and candor, high and low culture. This staggering portrait of an anti-heroine's death confirms Elisa Albert as a "witty, incisive" (*Variety*) and even "wonder-inducing" writer (*Time Out New York*).

ABOUT THE AUTHOR: **Elisa Albert** is the author of the short story collection *How This Night is Different* and the novel *The Book of Dahlia*. She is currently editing an anthology about sibling relationships called *Freud's Blind Spot*, to be published in 2010. Albert is a founding editor of Jewcy.com and an adjunct assistant professor of creative writing at Columbia University.

1. What was your initial impression of Dahlia? Did your opinion change as the story progressed and significant details about her life experience were revealed? Why or why not?

2. What do you think about the idea that a positive attitude is the most important ingredient for a happy, healthy life? Many of us have had experiences with cancer, either personally or in our families. How has this dictate to be "positive" affected us and our loved ones? Is there a part of us that wants to kick and scream and complain and feel sorry for ourselves, even though we know it's not productive? Discuss your own experiences with illness. Does illness transform us? Why or why not?

3. On some level is Dahlia a little bit glad to have this terminal illness? Does she believe it lends weight and shape and meaning and confirmation to her enormous unhappiness?

4. How would you answer one of the novel's central questions: Is a seemingly "wasted" life worth mourning?

5. If you found her difficult to like in general, are there nevertheless things about Dahlia that you do find sympathetic? When we encounter a character with whom we don't totally identify, what can we learn about ourselves from our reactions?

6. What do you think is useful about art (literature, music, film, painting, photography) that is "depressing" or full of angst and pain? Do you think we can learn from "depressing" art, or should we want to see only happy things?

7. In what ways does a character like Dahlia make us confront our own fears and regrets? What role has resentment played in your own life, and how have you conquered it or struggled to conquer it?

8. How do you think our society as a whole deals with death? Are you satisfied or dissatisfied with the cultural and religious ideas about death that you've encountered? What are your own attitudes about and notions of death? How have these changed throughout your life? Is it something you think about often? Why or why not?

Elisa Albert is available to speak by phone to reading groups.
Please contact Jill Siegel—Jill.Siegel@simonandschuster.com

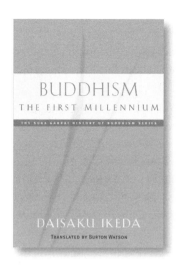

BUDDHISM
The First Millennium

AUTHOR: *Daisaku Ikeda*
Burton Watson

PUBLISHER: Middleway Press, 2009

WEBSITE: www.middlewaypress.com
www.ikedabooks.org

AVAILABLE IN:
Trade Paperback, 150 pages, $14.95
ISBN: 978-0-9779245-3-0

SUBJECT: Spirituality/Faith/Inspiration
(Nonfiction)

"This book provides a general overview of the first thousand years of one of the world's largest and most influential religions . . . and clearly defines the original ideas underlying Buddhism."—Los Angeles Times

SUMMARY: Beginning with the events immediately following the dark days after the death of Shakyamuni and continuing over a period of 1,000 years, this dynamic tome covers a vast and complex series of events and developments in the history of Buddhism. Through a thorough examination of its early development in India, a new light is cast on little-known aspects of Buddhist history and its relevance to the understanding of Buddhism today. Topics include the formation of the Buddhist canon, the cultural exchange between the East and West, and the spirit of the *Lotus Sutra*.

ABOUT THE AUTHORS: **Daisaku Ikeda** is the author and coauthor of more than 60 books on a wide range of topics, including the history of Buddhism and Buddhist philosophy. He is the founding president and leader of the Soka Gakkai International, one of the largest lay Buddhist organizations in the world. He is the recipient of the United Nations Peace Award, the Rosa Parks Humanitarian Award, and the International Tolerance Award of the Simon Wiesenthal Center.

Burton Watson is a translator of Chinese and Japanese literature. His translations include *Chuang Tzu: Basic Writings*, *The Lotus Sutra*, and *The Vimalakirti Sutra*, among others. He received the PEN Translation Prize in 1981.

1. *Buddhism, The First Millennium,* describes the spread of Buddhism in the centuries after the death of Shakyamuni. How did this religion flourish in its early years?

2. This book states that Shakyamuni left no writings to his disciples. Daisaku Ikeda describes how the basic principles and ideas of Buddhism were passed down through his followers, primarily by memory, word of mouth, and practice. Discuss how this is thought to have happened and how this compares to what you know of other religions.

3. This book describes a schism in Buddhist schools approximately one hundred years after the death of Shakyamuni. How did this affect the spread of Buddhism?

4. King Ashoka is presented as one of the most influential early Buddhist practitioners. How did his beliefs change the role of government? What was his legacy?

5. Discuss the importance of *The Questions of King Milinda.*

6. The author states that "Christianity and Buddhism are alike in preaching to all humankind a universal message about how one ought to live." Discuss similarities and differences that you see between the Buddhist and Christian teachings.

7. The German philosopher Karl Jaspers wrote, "What the Buddha taught was not a system of epistemology but a way of salvation." How did Mahayana Buddhism embody this in its writings five hundred years after the death of Shakyamuni?

8. Discuss the importance of the *Lotus Sutra.*

9. Nagarjuna has been called the second Buddha. How important are his writings to the spread of Buddhism to East Asia? Discuss his theory of non-substantiality.

10. The author states that Buddhism was never intended to be just a program of study. "The only way to understand Buddhism is through the experience and wisdom acquired through actual practice." Is this true today?

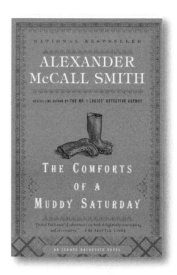

COMFORTS OF A MUDDY SATURDAY

AUTHOR: *Alexander McCall Smith*

PUBLISHER: Anchor Books, 2009

WEBSITE: www.ReadingGroupCenter.com
www.alexandermccallsmith.com

AVAILABLE IN:
Trade Paperback, 272 pages, $14.00
ISBN: 978-0-307-38707-3

SUBJECT: Mystery/Family/Women's Lives
(Fiction)

"Offers tantalizing glimpses of Edinburgh's complex character and a nice, long look into the beautiful mind of a thinking woman."—The New York Times Book Review

"Virtue and truth triumph. . . . If you enjoy discussing the big truths and thinking about thinking, you will enjoy The Comforts of a Muddy Saturday.*"*
—The Providence Journal

SUMMARY: In the delectable fifth installment of the bestselling adventures of Isabel Dalhousie, our cherished inquisitive heroine returns to investigate a medical mystery.

A doctor's career has been ruined by allegations of medical fraud and Isabel cannot ignore what may be a miscarriage of justice. Would a respected doctor make such a grave mistake? If not, what explains the death of the patient? Clearly, an investigation is in order. Meanwhile, there is her baby Charlie, who needs looking after; her niece Cat who needs someone to mind her deli; and a mysterious composer who has latched on to Jamie, making Isabel decidedly uncomfortable. Whatever the problem, whatever the case, we know we can count on Isabel's instincts to help her find the right solution.

ABOUT THE AUTHOR: **Alexander McCall Smith** is the author of the international phenomenon The *No. 1 Ladies' Detective Agency* series, the *Isabel Dalhousie* Series, the *Portuguese Irregular Verbs* series, and the *44 Scotland Street* series. He is professor emeritus of medical law at the University of Edinburgh in Scotland and has served on many national and international bodies concerned with bioethics.

1. At a somewhat dull dinner party, Isabel is engaged in a conversation about happiness with a doctor seated next to her. She argues, "most people are reasonably happy;" he argues that "most people are unhappy in one way or another" [p. 12]. With what evidence does he support his opinion? With whom do you agree, and why?

2. Why does Isabel feel herself to be at a disadvantage when the composer Nick Smart is present? What do these scenes indicate about Jamie and Isabel's status as a couple?

3. Why does Isabel treat the submission of an article by Christopher Dove so carefully? What feelings does she need to overcome in order to handle the situation? Does she do the right thing, or would it have been more satisfying if she had indulged her less noble instincts [pp. 24–29]?

4. Most of the novel is narrated from Isabel's point of view, but occasionally we are given access to the thoughts of Jamie [pp. 40, 45]. What would the story be like if Smith were to distribute access to the main characters' thoughts more equally? Would this have a positive or negative effect on your reading experience?

5. Why does Eddie lie to Isabel regarding the money? Do you agree with Isabel that a lie is harmful, and that "truth [is] built into the world" [p. 145]?

6. Jamie reveals to Isabel that he's been meeting with Nick Smart because he's been working on composing a musical piece for Isabel, and Isabel realizes "she had misread everything—again" [p. 134]. What does Isabel need to learn about Jamie, and about herself?

7. Where, and in what kinds of situations, are the moments of comedy in the story? How would you describe Isabel's sense of humor?

8. One of the things that is perhaps unusual in this series is the presence of "little snatches of poetry." Does the presence of poetry enhance these novels, and if so, how?

9. How are the Isabel Dalhousie novels not typical of the mystery genre?

10. What does the revelation that Jamie is alienated from his family suggest (if anything) for his future with Charlie and Isabel [p. 217]?

11. Discuss the domestic "muddy Saturday" scene with which the story ends [pp. 237–40]. What does this scene suggest about the bonds between Isabel, Jamie and Charlie?

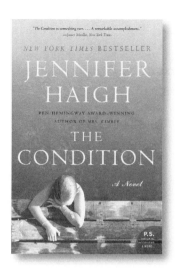

THE CONDITION

AUTHOR: *Jennifer Haigh*

PUBLISHER: Harper Perennial, 2009

WEBSITE: www.harperperennial.com
www.jenniferhaigh.com

AVAILABLE IN:
Trade Paperback, 416 pages, $14.99
ISBN: 978-0-060-75579-9

SUBJECT: Family/Relationships/
Love & Romance (Fiction)

"[Haigh] looks unflinchingly at family ties—the kind that limit and the kind that can actually liberate. The Condition *is a satisfying feat of literary choreography."—***Wall Street Journal**

"Haigh's characters are layered and authentic. Moreover, one would have to have a heart of stone not to care for them and follow their small sagas. . . . Haigh is such a gifted chronicler of the human condition."
—Chris Bohjalian, *Washington Post Book World*

SUMMARY: In the summer of 1976, during their annual retreat on Cape Cod, the McKotch family came apart. Now, twenty years after daughter Gwen was diagnosed with Turner's syndrome—a rare genetic condition that keeps her trapped forever in the body of a child—eminent scientist Frank McKotch is divorced from his pedigreed wife, Paulette. Eldest son Billy, a successful cardiologist, lives a life built on secrets and compromise. His brother Scott awakened from a pot-addled adolescence to a soul-killing job and a regrettable marriage. And Gwen spurns all social interaction until, well into her thirties, she falls in love for the first time. *The Condition* explores the power of family mythologies—the self-delusions, denials, and inescapable truths that forever bind fathers and mothers and siblings.

ABOUT THE AUTHOR: **Jennifer Haigh** is the author of *The New York Times* bestseller *Baker Towers* and *Mrs. Kimble*, which won the PEN/ Hemingway Award for debut fiction and was a finalist for the Book Sense Book of the Year. Both novels were number one Book Sense picks. Her fiction has appeared in *Granta, Ploughshares, Good Housekeeping* and elsewhere. She lives in the Boston area.

1. Discuss the significance of the book's title. What else might it refer to other than Gwen's Turner's syndrome?

2. In what ways does Gwen's condition reverberate throughout the McKotch family? What do Frank and Paulette's differing opinions about how to treat Gwen's condition reveal about their personalities and also about their relationship?

3. Frank often compares his working-class background in a Pennsylvania mining town with Paulette's pedigreed family, musing that everything comes down to upbringing. How does his children's upbringing affect the paths they take in life? Was Frank a bad father, as Paulette seemed to believe?

4. Why does Gwen distance herself from her family both physically and emotionally? Why does she ultimately decide to forgive Rico and Scott but not her mother?

5. Do you agree with Paulette's decision to send Scott to St. Raphael to bring Gwen home? Why is it so difficult for Paulette to believe that a man might be attracted to Gwen? Is she merely being a protective mother?

6. Gwen ends up living on St. Raphael, worlds away from her isolated life in Pittsburgh and Concord before that. What does she find on the Caribbean island that she hasn't anywhere else? Why does she reconcile with Rico?

7. By the time the family reconvenes at the Captain's House, what realizations has Scott come to about his life—professionally and romantically, as well as his role as a father? In what ways have the others changed by the time of the reunion?

8. Sense of place is an important theme in *The Condition*. How do the opening scenes at the Captain's House set the tone for the rest of the novel? What do the main characters' living spaces, from Paulette's 200-year-old Concord house to Billy's meticulously decorated New York City apartment, reveal about them?

9. Jennifer Haigh unfolds the narrative from the alternating perspectives of Frank, Paulette, and their three children. In what ways did this enhance your reading of the story?

10. If you have read Jennifer Haigh's previous novels, *Baker Towers* and *Mrs. Kimble*, discuss the similarities and differences between those two books and *The Condition*.

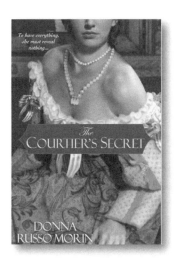

THE COURTIER'S SECRET

AUTHOR: *Donna Russo Morin*

PUBLISHER: Kensington Books, 2009

WEBSITE: www.donnarussomorin.com
www.kensingtonbooks.com

AVAILABLE IN:
Trade Paperback, 384 pages, $14.00
ISBN: 978-0-7582-2691-4

SUBJECT: Women's Lives/Intrigue/
Adventure (Historical Fiction)

Exquisitely done . . . fabulous . . . unforgettable characters."
—**Marilyn Rondeau**

"Compelling . . . brings vividly to life the constrained life of the noble Frenchwoman."—**Allie Bates, author of** *Earthchild*

SUMMARY: France, 1680. Louis XIV, the Sun King, is at the height of his power. The court at Versailles is a paradise for privileged young women. Jeanne Yvette Mas Du Bois is unlike most other courtiers and her thirst for knowledge often incurs her father's brutal wrath. But her uncle encourages Jeanne's independence, secretly teaching her fencing in the palace's labyrinthine basement. When two of the king's Musketeers are beset by criminals who are mere feet from Jeanne's fencing lesson, she intervenes, saving one of the Musketeers' lives. Hidden behind her mask, Jeanne is mistaken for a man. As "Jean Luc," Jeanne is admitted to an inner circle where she learns of an assassination plot against the Queen. Now, with the Queen in jeopardy, and her own double life making her privy to the tangled intrigues at court, Jeanne is in a powerful—yet increasingly perilous—position. Brimming with lush period detail and vivid, unforgettable characters, *The Courtier's Secret* takes readers into a fascinating, intriguing world of pageantry, adventure, betrayals, and secrets.

ABOUT THE AUTHOR: **Donna Russo Morin** is a graduate of the University of Rhode Island, where she obtained two degrees. In addition to writing, editing, and teaching, Donna dabbles as a model and actor, using yet another imaginary world to help support her real one. Donna's two sons, Devon and Dylan, are her greatest works in progress.

1. How would you characterize Jeanne du Bois? What is it about her that makes her unique from other women of her era? How do these differences affect her life, both positively and negatively?

2. In Chapter One, Jeanne describes her frustrations at the limited choices in her life to her mother, saying, "I cannot bear a life where the most momentous decisions I have to make are what to wear and what to serve. It is too meaningless and trivial. I want to learn things, study, be a part of the world." Do you feel the women of today experience the same problems? In what way is it the same? How have things changed? How does Jeanne's attitude frame the entire story?

3. How do Jeanne and her friends Olympe and Lynette differ in their desires for their lives? How are they all representative of the women of their era? In what way do they all ultimately receive what they want?

4. What does Jeanne mean when she says, in Chapter Two, "How can my love of God be measured by how deeply I curtsey to the nuns?" What other events and statements reveal her inner feelings of religion, and how are they juxtaposed to her feelings about God?

5. Why do you think Jeanne's Uncle Jules helps her with her disguise, enabling and encouraging her to lead a double life?

6. Athénaïs, the Marquise de Montespan, was one of the few married women to become a King's mistress. What factors allowed it? What in her past ignites the fear of François Scarron in King Louis' life?

7. Is it just an advantageous match Gaston demands for his daughter or is there more to his insistence upon Jeanne marrying Percy de Polignac? What other advantages were there for arranged marriages? Could such a practice be possible in today's society?

8. To what extent does the particular time in history in which the story is set influence the tone of the story?

9. In Chapter Eighteen, Jeanne describes the frightened look of the deer as it is hunted down. What does the deer symbolize for her, and in what ways?

10. As Jeanne says good-bye to "Jean-Luc," she acknowledges that she will miss him, but that she no longer needs him. In what way did she "need" him before? What changed to dispel her need?

11. What is it about the tales of the Three Musketeers that is so enduring? Are there any similarities to another group of like-minded warriors in modern-day stories? How are they alike?

12. The truth of this story lies in the internal conflict raging within Jeanne. What is that conflict?

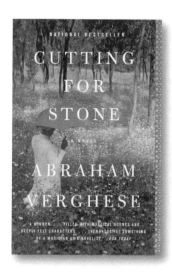

CUTTING FOR STONE

AUTHOR: *Abraham Verghese*

PUBLISHER: Vintage Books, January 2010

WEBSITE: www.ReadingGroupCenter.com
www.abrahamverghese.com

AVAILABLE IN:
Trade Paperback, 560 pages, $15.95
ISBN: 978-0-375-71436-8

SUBJECT: Family/Culture & World
Issues/Personal Challenges (Fiction)

"To exhilarate you. . . . A saga about love, medicine, and exile, this debut reads like a modern Odyssey *as it follows twin boys born in an Ethiopian mission hospital as they search for the man presumed to be their father."*
—*Good Housekeeping*

SUMMARY: Marion and Shiva Stone are twin brothers born of a secret union between a beautiful Indian nun and a brash British surgeon at a mission hospital in Addis Ababa. Orphaned by their mother's death in childbirth and their father's disappearance, the twins come of age as Ethiopia hovers on the brink of revolution. Yet it will be love, not politics—their passion for the same woman—that will tear them apart and force Marion to flee his homeland. He makes his way to America, finding refuge in his work as an intern at an underfunded, overcrowded New York City hospital. When the past catches up to him—nearly destroying him—Marion must entrust his life to the two men he thought he trusted least in the world: the surgeon father who abandoned him and the brother who betrayed him.

An unforgettable journey into one man's remarkable life, and an epic story about the power, intimacy, and curious beauty of the work of healing others.

ABOUT THE AUTHOR: **Abraham Verghese** is also the author of *The Tennis Partner*, a *New York Times* Notable Book, and *My Own Country*, a National Book Critics Circle finalist. He is a professor of internal medicine at Stanford University. He lives in Palo Alto, California.

1. Abraham Verghese has said that his ambition in writing *Cutting for Stone* was to "tell a great story, an old-fashioned, truth-telling story." In what ways is *Cutting for Stone* an old-fashioned story—and what does it share with the great novels of the nineteenth century? What essential human truths does it convey?

2. Contrast the attitudes of Hema, Ghosh, Marion, Shiva, and Thomas Stone toward their work. What draws each of them to the practice of medicine? How are they affected, emotionally and otherwise, by the work they do?

3. What important differences does *Cutting for Stone* reveal about the way illness is viewed and treated in Ethiopia and in the United States?

4. How does Verghese use medical detail to create tension and surprise? What do his depictions of dramatic surgeries share with film and television hospital dramas—and yet how are they different?

5. To what extent does the story of Thomas Stone's childhood soften Marion's judgment of him? How does Thomas's suffering as a child, the illness of his parents, and his own illness help to explain why he abandons Shiva and Marion at their birth? How should Thomas finally be judged?

6. In what important ways does Marion come to resemble his father, although he grows up without him? How does Marion grow and change over the course of the novel?

7. A passionate, unique love affair sets *Cutting for Stone* in motion. How does the relationship between Sister Mary Joseph Praise and Thomas Stone affect the lives of Shiva and Marion, Hema and Ghosh, Matron and everyone else at Missing? What do you think Verghese is trying to say about the nature of love and loss?

8. What do the women who come to Missing seeking medical treatment reveal about what life is like for women in Ethiopia?

9. What is the key to Ghosh's contentment? What makes him such a good father, doctor, and teacher? What wisdom does he impart to Marion?

10. Almost all of the characters in *Cutting for Stone* are living in some sort of exile, self-imposed or forced. What do you think this novel says about exile and the immigrant experience? How does exile change these characters, and what do they find themselves missing the most about home?

DEAR AMERICAN AIRLINES

AUTHOR: *Jonathan Miles*

PUBLISHER: Mariner Books, 2009

WEBSITE: www.hmhbooks.com
www.dearamericanairlines.com

AVAILABLE IN:
Trade Paperback, 192 pages, $13.95
ISBN: 978-0-547-23790-9

SUBJECT: Humor/Intrigue/Family (Fiction)

"Wildly entertaining . . . not just philosophically but emotionally rewarding."—**Richard Russo, The New York Times Book Review**

"A brilliant conception. . . . Mr. Miles is a superb writer."—**Steve Weinberg, Dallas Morning News**

"A thoroughly amusing and ultimately poignant howl about life's injustices . . . appealingly loose . . . emotionally wrenching."—**Scott Morris, The Wall Street Journal**

"Tender and corrosively funny."—**Tina Jordan, Entertainment Weekly**

SUMMARY: When Bennie Ford's flight is cancelled, he finds himself stranded at Chicago's O'Hare airport with the growing realization that he will miss his daughter's wedding. Worse, he's breaking their deal: that they will spend time getting to know one another before his daughter, whom he hasn't seen or contacted in more than twenty years, will allow him to walk her down the aisle. Frustrated, irate, and helpless, Bennie does the only thing he can: he puts pen to paper. But what begins as a hilariously excoriating demand for a refund soon becomes a lament for a life gone awry, for years misspent, talent wasted, and happiness lost.

ABOUT THE AUTHOR: **Jonathan Miles** is the cocktails columnist for *The New York Times*. His journalism, essays, and literary criticism have appeared in many publications, including *The New York Times* Book Review, *GQ, The New York Observer*, and the *Oxford American*. A former longtime resident of Oxford, Mississippi but now lives in New York.

1. Why do you think the author chose the story of Walenty, a fictional soldier in the novel Bennie is translating, as a foil for Bennie's own story? Compare and contrast these two protagonists. For example, Walenty struggles with the amputation of his leg and its replacement with a wooden one. What does Bennie say has been amputated from his own life?

2. Bennie muses that, "the right word matters . . . the wrong ones infect, spread disease. Words are everything." How have words held significance throughout Bennie's life? Compare and contrast the way he has used or abused spoken words versus written words, and the way each has influenced him.

3. *Dear American Airlines* is filled with allusions to traps and escapes. Identify some of these moments, both real and metaphoric. Who feels that they are trapped? Who longs for escape? Discuss how these feelings play a role in the lives of the characters that express or experience them.

4. Bennie relays a passage from the novel he is translating in which Walenty explains to a New Zealand officer of Trieste: "This is someplace else." But the colonel replies, "Not anymore." What does this exchange mean? Why does Walenty so badly need Trieste to be "someplace else?" Is Bennie also looking for "someplace else?" Do you think he finds it? Why or why not?

5. Bennie's mistakes seem to be bigger than mere missteps: knowing his family history [note: alcoholism and bipolar disorder frequently go hand in hand], how much control do you think Bennie has really had in his life? Are you more or less sympathetic to his character given the details of his childhood? Explain your opinion.

6. The format of the novel is unique but familiar: a long, continuous letter written by Bennie to complain and request a refund from American Airlines, whose cancellation of several flights has left hundreds of people stranded at O'Hare airport. Why do you think the author chose this format? How does this structure contribute to your reading experience?

7. Bennie ultimately concludes that maybe there are no better fates than the path you've chosen. "You can't escape what you are be it a possum or poet. Maybe you get what you get," he writes. What do you think?

8. The novel concludes with the statement, "There was no Free State of Trieste and there never could be." What is the significance of this moment for Walenty, and likewise for Bennie? Do you think Bennie has changed over the course of the novel? Why does he choose to forego his refund after all?

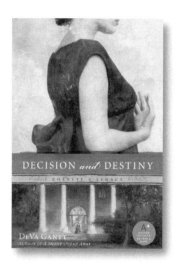

DECISION AND DESTINY
Colette's Legacy

AUTHOR: *DeVa Gantt*

PUBLISHER: Avon A, 2009

WEBSITE: www.avonbooks.com
web.mac.com/devagantt

AVAILABLE IN:
Trade Paperback, 400 pages, $13.99
ISBN: 978-0-061-57825-0

SUBJECT: Adventure/Love & Romance/
Intrigue (Historical Fiction)

SUMMARY: A spellbinding saga of a remarkable American family . . .

The beautiful, frail Colette Duvoisin trusted governess Charmaine Ryan with her worries, her dreams, and the care of her beloved children. But now Colette is gone—leaving her three young ones devastated . . . and the house of Duvoisin in turmoil.

To her children's horror, their father, the enigmatic Frederic Duvoisin, weds his mistress and sister-in-law, Agatha, soon after their mother's untimely death. A scheming and dangerous adversary, Agatha has no love for her predecessor's offspring, ruthlessly wielding her newly won power while guarding her own dark secrets. Meanwhile, a rivalry between Colette's stepsons—suave Paul and cynical John—is reignited, drawing battle lines among family, friends, and servants. When Frederic suddenly emerges from his self-imposed isolation, he touches off a struggle for patriarchal supremacy that threatens to lay the entire Duvoisin empire to waste. At the center of the storm is innocent Charmaine, who must come to terms with shattering truths about the family she once believed she knew—and decide who among them deserves her admiration, her derision, her devotion . . . and her heart.

ABOUT THE AUTHOR: **DeVa Gantt** is a pseudonym for coauthor sisters Deb and Val Gantt. Valerie and Debra were born and raised in New Jersey, where the Colette Trilogy—commencing with *A Silent Ocean Away*—was conceived. Presently, they live in New York. Both women are married, have children, and maintain full-time careers.

1. What is the significance of the title. Discuss ways in which both decisions and destiny each play a role in the characters behaviors.

2. Although the character of Colette has died, her legacy also determines the fate of many of the Duvoisin family—especially Frederic. Discuss ways in which Colette's life and fate still influence the family itself.

3. What are Frederic's true motives? He appears contrite, but he continues to provoke members of the family, especially John.

4. Humor is effectively employed throughout this novel. Discuss ways in which it lessens the turmoil of the book.

5. There are elements of the supernatural and indications of a ghost wandering the house. Do you believe that Colette's spirit is still haunting the home? Do you personally believe in the presence of the supernatural?

6. *Decision and Destiny* is part of a trilogy. Do you like novels with sequels and connecting characters or would you have preferred this to have been one long novel?

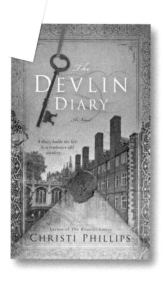

THE DEVLIN DIARY

AUTHOR: *Christi Phillips*

PUBLISHER: Pocket Books, April 2010

WEBSITE: www.simonandschuster.com
www.christi-phillips.com

AVAILABLE IN:
Trade Paperback, 384 pages, $15.00
ISBN: 978-1-4165-2740-4

SUBJECT: History/Mystery/Adventure
(Fiction)

"Phillips's command of period detail and her sure touch with emotional relationships help make this a standout."—Publishers Weekly (**Starred Review**)

SUMMARY: Teaching history at Trinity College, Cambridge, is Claire Donovan's dream come true—until one of her colleagues is found dead on the banks of the River Cam. The only key to the professor's unsolved murder is the seventeenth-century diary kept by his last research subject, Hannah Devlin, physician to the king's mistress. As Claire and historian Andrew Kent follow the clues Devlin left behind, they discover the life of an extraordinary woman and a hidden conspiracy involving King Charles II which might still have deadly consequences today.

A suspenseful and richly satisfying tale brimming with sharply observed historical detail, *The Devlin Diary* brings past and present to vivid life. With wit and grace, Christi Phillips holds readers spellbound with an extraordinary novel of secrets, obsession, and the haunting power of the past.

ABOUT THE AUTHOR: **Christi Phillips** is the author of *The Rossetti Letter*, which has been translated into six foreign languages. Her research combines a few of her favorite things: old books, libraries, and travel. When she's not rummaging around in an archive or exploring the historic heart of a European city, she lives with her husband in the San Francisco Bay Area, where she is at work on her next novel, set in France.

1. What is your first impression of Claire Donovan? What did you think of Andrew Kent at the beginning of the novel? How did your feelings about these characters change throughout the story? What were major turning points for you?

2. *The Devlin Diary* has two major settings: the court of Charles II and present-day Trinity College, Cambridge. Each of these places has unique characteristics, yet they share a few similarities. How are these two communities similar and how are they different?

3. Claire Donovan and Hannah Devlin are both strong women in predominantly male cultures. How does each woman approach difficult or delicate situations throughout the book? Compare and contrast Claire's and Hannah's situations and personalities. Which female character did you relate to more? Why?

4. What motivates Hannah Devlin to step beyond the circumscribed role of a respectable woman in seventeenth-century London society? What does Hannah appear to sacrifice by flouting society's conventions?

5. Lord Arlington tells Hannah "You are a woman, after all" and Hannah thinks "A woman, after all. Something inferior to man is his implication—what all men imply when they speak of the 'weaker' sex, the 'gentler' sex, a woman's 'modesty'." Do you believe that either Claire or Hannah is a feminist? Why or why not?

6. Many of the characters in this novel harbor secrets from others and many characters are not entirely honest with themselves. Which characters in both the historical and contemporary stories seem straightforward and at ease with themselves and their desires?

7. Ralph Montagu and Edward Strathern, two very different male characters, are attracted to Hannah Devlin. Do the same aspects of Hannah's character attract each man? How did your opinion of each man change during the course of the novel?

8. What is the role of Theophilus Ravenscroft in the novel? Do you believe the author inserted him in the historical story merely to provide some comic relief? Does he have a counterpart in the contemporary story?

9. How does the author use language and imagery to bring the characters to life? Did the novel's characters or style remind you of another novel in any way?

10. Whose story is *The Devlin Diary*? If you had to pick one, is it Claire's story or is it Hannah's? Why?

11. How did this book touch your life? Did it inspire you to do or learn something new?

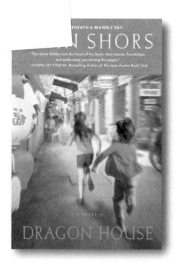

DRAGON HOUSE

AUTHOR: *John Shors*

PUBLISHER: New American Library, 2009

WEBSITE: www.dragonhousebook.com
www.penguin.com

Available in:
Trade Paperback, 384 pages, $15.00
ISBN: 978-0-451-22785-0

SUBJECT: Relationships/Culture & World Issues/Personal Discovery (Fiction)

"In a large cast of appealing characters, the street children are the heart of this book; their talents, friendships, and perils keep you turning the pages."—**Karen Joy Fowler, *The New York Times* bestselling author of *The Jane Austen Book Club***

"All of his characters—hustlers, humanitarians, street children— carry wounds, visible or otherwise. And in the cacophony of their voices, he asks that most essential question: 'How can we be better?'"
—**David Oliver Relin, co-author of *Three Cups of Tea***

SUMMARY: From the critically acclaimed author of *Beneath a Marble Sky* and *Beside a Burning Sea*—the new novel from "a master storyteller" (Amy Tan) set in contemporary Asia. *Dragon House* tells the tale of Iris and Noah—two Americans who, as a way of healing their own painful pasts, open a center to house and educate Vietnamese street children. In the slums of a city that has known little but war for generations, Iris and Noah befriend children who dream of nothing more than of going to school, having a home, and being loved. Learning from the poorest of the poor, Iris and Noah find themselves reborn. *Dragon House* brings together East and West, war and peace, and celebrates the resilience of the human spirit.

ABOUT THE AUTHOR: **John Shors** traveled extensively throughout Asia after graduating from Colorado College in 1991. He now divides his time between writing and spending time with his wife and two young children.

A portion of the proceeds from this book's sales will be donated to the Blue Dragon Children's Foundation. To learn more, visit www.bdcf.org.

1. What compelled you to read *Dragon House*?

2. What did you enjoy most about the novel?

3. Were you aware that so many children around the world are homeless?

4. Which character did you like the most? Why?

5. Do you think John Shors tried to draw comparisons between the Vietnam War and the Iraq War? If so, why?

6. If you have read John Shors' earlier novels (*Beneath a Marble Sky* and *Beside a Burning Sea*), how do you think he has changed as a writer, if at all?

7. What did you think of Loc? Why do you think the author chose to make him a former street child?

8. Could you tell that John Shors had traveled extensively in Vietnam? Do think it's important for writers to visit the places that they bring to life?

9. The author talks a lot about "dragons" in his novel. What do you think dragons symbolize in the story?

10. Did you enjoy Minh's character more when he was silent or when he spoke? Why?

11. Would you like to read a sequel to *Dragon House*? If a sequel were written, what do you think would happen in it?

12. What do you enjoy most about John Shors' writing style?

Want to connect with the author? John Shors is available to speak with your book club. Please contact Michele Langley at Michele.Langley@us.penguingroup.com for more information.

THE END

AUTHOR: *Salvatore Scibona*

PUBLISHER: Riverhead Books, October 2009

WEBSITE: www.theendnovel.com
www.penguin.com

AVAILABLE IN:
Trade Paperback, 336 pages, $16.00
ISBN: 978-1-59448-405-6

SUBJECT: Family/Social Issues/Identity
(Fiction)

The National Book Award Finalist

Winner of the 2009 New York Public Library Young Lions Fiction Award

"Exquisitely rendered."—Los Angeles Times

"Breathtaking . . . Think not only Faulkner, but also T. S. Eliot, Virginia Woolf, Gertrude Stein and James Joyce."—Cleveland Plain Dealer

"Engulfing . . . Entangled . . . Memento *meets* Augie March *. . . Didion meets Hitchcock."—Esquire*

SUMMARY: It is August 15, 1953, the day of a boisterous and unwieldy street carnival in Elephant Park, an Italian immigrant enclave in northern Ohio. As the festivities reach a riotous pitch and billow into the streets, five members of the community labor under the weight of a terrible secret. As these floundering souls collide, one day of calamity and consequence sheds light on a half century of their struggles, their follies, and their pride. And slowly, it becomes clear that buried deep in the hearts of these five exquisitely drawn characters is the long-silenced truth about the crime that twisted each of their worlds.

ABOUT THE AUTHOR: **Salvatore Scibona's** fiction has been published in *The Threepenny Review* and the *Pushcart Prize anthology*. A graduate of the Iowa Writer's Workshop, he is the writing coordinator at the Fine Arts Work Center in Provincetown, Massachusetts.

1. Although the novel follows the lives of five unique characters, why do you think we meet Rocco LaGrassa first among them? Is he more sympathetic than the others? How does his situation—abandoned by his family and on a quest to find them—resonate with the greater themes of the book?

2. When Rocco is at Niagara Falls, he is certain that he and the ice cream man share a moment of mutual recognition, although the latter denies it. Why is the moment so bright in Rocco's memory? What do you think this scene illumines about the role of memory in the rest of the book?

3. Mrs. Marini describes her breasts as "withered medlars . . . unique among fruits in that it is inedible until it starts to rot." It is a description that could be applied to Mrs. Marini herself. What do you think Mrs. Marini is trying to say about herself? Could anyone else in the novel be similarly described?

4. Why does Patrizia stay on at the grape farm after Umberto abandons it to return to Italy? What do you think Francesco means when he calls Ashtabula County's soil "too good . . . to grow respectable wine grapes"? How might this sentiment also apply to the neighborhood of Elephant Park?

5. In what way is Ciccio's shame intertwined with his sense that "he had become a grown man"? Do you think this sense of shame can be linked to something else in Ciccio's life? In Lina's? How is his experience in America different from Rocco's? Ciccio's?

6. Despite the circumstances of her departure, Lina comes back to Elephant Park. Why do you think she came back, even when the place haunts her? Was it only for Ciccio?

7. The day of the carnival is saturated with an underlying sense of racial menace yet no act of violence is actually committed against the African-American characters. What is the role of race in the novel? How else is it manifested in the story?

EVENING IS THE WHOLE DAY

AUTHOR: *Preeta Samarasan*

PUBLISHER: Mariner Books, 2009

WEBSITE: www.hmhbooks.com
www.preetasamarasan.com

AVAILABLE IN:
Trade Paperback, 352 pages, $13.95
ISBN: 978-0-547-23789-3

SUBJECT: Family/Culture & World Issues/
Intrigue (Fiction)

*"A complex web of public and private histories shared by an Indian immigrant family is painstakingly examined in the ambitious first novel. . . . [Samarasan] scores impressively with the creation of an intimate, gossipy omniscient narrative voice that's the perfect vehicle for her slowly unfolding, intricately layered story."—**Kirkus Review***

SUMMARY: When the Rajasekharan family's rubber-plantation servant girl is dismissed for unnamed crimes, it is only the latest in a series of precipitous losses that have shaken six-year-old Aasha's life. In the space of several weeks her grandmother passed away under mysterious circumstances, and Uma, her older sister, left for Columbia University, forever. Aasha is left stranded in a family, and a country, slowly going to pieces.

Circling through years of family history to arrive at the moment of Uma's departure, *Evening is the Whole Day* illuminates in heartbreaking detail one Indian immigrant family's layers of secrets and lies, while exposing the complex underbelly of Malaysia itself. Sweeping in scope, exuberantly lyrical and masterfully constructed, Preeta Samarasan's debut is a mesmerizing and vital achievement, perfect as a reading group selection, and sure to earn her a place alongside Arundhati Roy and Zadie Smith.

ABOUT THE AUTHOR: **Preeta Samarasan** was born in Malaysia and moved to the United States to finish high school at the United World College U.S.A. and attend Hamilton College. She currently lives in central France with her husband and dog.

1. How does the Big House bear witness to changes in the family, to the history of the land, and to changing politics? Describe how it also witness power struggles between rich and poor, British, Indian, Chinese and Malaysian, the traditional and the new.

2. Why do you think the author refers to the colonial rulers instead of simply comparing Ipoh to the United Kingdom? Do you think the Rajasekharan family identifies more with the British rulers, or the natives?

3. Amma keeps Aasha and Suresh at the table to witness Chellam's departure, and Appa interprets this as her way of teaching a lesson: how people can turn against you even after you've helped them. Identify other examples or situations that might offer proof of the same lesson and discuss your feelings about this sentiment.

4. As Aasha longingly follows the "new Uma" around the house, she describes an "aching, violent dusk that has come to seem the permanent state of the whole year." Why do you think she feels this way? Does this shed any light on the book's title? Why or why not?

5. Watching Uma pack for her departure to America, Aasha thinks about "what people take and what they leave behind" and about "how much room there is in a suitcase." Discuss the significance of these thoughts as they relate to the events of the novel.

6. How do you think Amma's humble beginnings affect her worldview, and later, her judgment of Chellam and the servants? Does her own past make her more empathetic or expectant of her servants?

7. When Paati disapproves of Amma, Appa demands, "you will treat her with the same respect you owe any human being." This exemplifies his beginnings as an idealist, wanting to change the world. Why do you think he gives up these ideals, and what does he gain and/or loose?

8. Does Appa's career of "believing in guilt" make it easier for him forgive it at home? What crimes is he, himself, guilty of? How might those wrongdoings affect his resolve as a prosecutor?

9. Paati promises Uma to always take care of her. Discuss why Uma feels Paati has broken this promise and Uma's subsequent reaction.

10. Appa successfully convicts the wrong person of rape and murder. Over and over we find members of the family taking their frustrations out on the wrong people. Identify some examples of misplaced frustrations and discuss how the underlying themes of guilt versus innocence, truth versus lies, and fact versus rumor relate.

11. Describe how you think that story would differ if told from the perspectives of Aasha, Suresh, Amma, and Chellam.

EVERY LAST CUCKOO

AUTHOR: *Kate Maloy*

PUBLISHER: Algonquin Books, 2009

WEBSITE: www.algonquin.com
www.katemaloy.com

AVAILABLE IN
Trade Paperback, 304 pages, $13.95
ISBN: 978-1-56512-675-6

SUBJECT: Family/Women's Lives/Personal Discovery (Fiction)

"Maloy's novel grabs the reader by the heart. . . . In this portrait of a long and loving marriage, [she] gives us a real human family, with all its love and conflict and change, as well as a look at the richness that can come with age."—**The New Orleans Times-Picayune**

"A truly engrossing novel. . . . This lovely tale depicts the surprises and changes that come with aging. . . . An excellent book club selection."—**Library Journal**

SUMMARY: Sarah Lucas imagined the rest of her days would be spent living peacefully in her rural Vermont home, in the steadfast company of her husband. But after Charles dies suddenly, seventy-five-year-old Sarah is left inconsolably alone—until a variety of wayward souls come seeking shelter in her big, empty home. As Sarah and this unruly flock form a family of sorts, they nurture and protect one another, discovering their unsuspected strengths and courage.

In the tradition of Jane Smiley and Sue Miller, Kate Maloy has crafted a wise and gratifying novel about a woman who gracefully accepts a surprising new role just when she thinks her best years are behind her.

ABOUT THE AUTHOR: **Kate Maloy** is the author of the memoir *A Stone Bridge North: Reflections in a New Life.* Her work has been published online in *Literary Mama* and *VerbSap* and in the *Readerville Journal*, the *Kenyon Review*, and the anthologies *For Keeps* and *Choice.* She lives with her husband on the central coast of Oregon.

1. We first see Sarah Lucas as she is racing into the Vermont winter woods on the heels of her dog Sylvie. What was your first impression of this 75-year-old woman?

2. What do you think the woods represents to Sarah? How has her relationship to nature changed since her childhood? What caused it to change?

3. Rural Vermont is rugged, poor, and sparsely populated. How do you think this environment has affected Sarah throughout her life?

4. Sarah's long marriage to Charles was mainly happy and successful, but it did have rough periods. How did the two of them weather these times without lingering resentments?

5. After Charles dies, Sarah goes numb, avoids people, and doesn't even cry. What breaks into her suspended state? Once her numbness wears off, does her grief take on new aspects and forms of expression, or does she just set grief aside and get on with things?

6. What do you see as milestones on Sarah's pathway to a new life and perhaps even a new identity? Have you ever reinvented yourself? What were your milestones?

7. On impulse, Sarah takes Charles's old camera with her on a late-winter walk. Eventually, photography helps to change the way she sees. What does she examine with her new eyes?

8. Why, over time, does Sarah enjoy taking increasingly puzzling and ambiguous photographs?

9. Charlotte and David respond very differently to Sarah's photographs. How do their responses reflect their relationships with her?

10. Sarah's view of the world is somewhat altered after hearing about the murder of Tess's husband and Mordechai's experiences in Israel. How do these things affect Sarah's actions and assumptions?

11. Why do you think Sarah agrees to take new people into her life?

12. What enables Sarah's teenage boarders—who had been so unhappy and even angry in their own homes—to calm down in Sarah's?

13. As the seasons change throughout the novel, so do all the characters' lives, both inner and outer. Sarah's changes are the most obvious and dramatic, but which of the other characters' lives changed the most?

14. What might Sarah have done differently in her encounter with Roger? How different might the outcome have been?

15. Throughout this novel we see natural hazards in the form of violent storms, life-threatening cold, and animal predation. We see human hazards such as domestic violence, murder, and warfare. What is the connection? Are humans given to violence or destruction because we are part of nature? Or can we choose otherwise?

FINDING NOUF

AUTHOR: *Zoë Ferraris*

PUBLISHER: Mariner Books, 2009

WEBSITE: www.hmhbooks.com
www.zoeferraris.com

AVAILABLE IN:
Trade Paperback, 320 pages, $13.95
ISBN: 978-0-547-23778-7

SUBJECT: Mystery/Family/Culture &
World Issues (Fiction)

"Ferraris offers up a fascinating peek into the lives and minds of devout Muslim men and women while serving up an engrossing mystery. . . . Highly recommended."—**Library Journal**

SUMMARY: When sixteen-year-old Nouf goes missing, her prominent family calls on Nayir al-Sharqi, a pious desert guide, to lead the search party. Ten days later, just as Nayir is about to give up in frustration, her body is discovered by anonymous desert travelers. But when the coroner's office determines that Nouf died not of dehydration but from drowning, and her family seems suspiciously uninterested in getting at the truth, Nayir takes it upon himself to find out what really happened.

He quickly realizes that if he wants to gain access to the hidden world of women, he will have to join forces with Katya Hijazi, a lab worker at the coroner's office who is bold enough to bare her face and to work in public. Their partnership challenges Nayir, as he confronts his desire for female companionship and the limitations imposed by his beliefs. Fast-paced and utterly transporting, *Finding Nouf* is a riveting literary mystery that offers an unprecedented window into Saudi Arabia and the lives of men and women there.

ABOUT THE AUTHOR: **Zoë Ferraris** moved to Saudi Arabia in the aftermath of the first gulf war to live with her then husband and his extended family of Saudi-Palestinian Bedouins, She has an MFA from Columbia University and currently lives in San Francisco.

1. What deeper meaning does the search for Nouf have for Nayir? Discuss the relevance of the title, *Finding Nouf.*
2. How do Muslim customs hinder Nayir and Katya in their investigation? How do these customs help the investigators?
3. Nayir's identity is almost entirely contingent on his modesty and righteousness. Do you think he overdoes it? If so, what might Nayir be compensating for? How do other Muslims in the novel, both men and women, seem to feel about his religious conservatism?
4. Find examples throughout the book of Nayir's longing for contact with, and insight into, womankind. Discuss how his opinions and impressions change or remain the same by the end of the novel.
5. The novel portrays various levels of seclusion in Saudi Arabian culture. Identify the ways in which people and groups are cut off from one another, both literally and figuratively, and examine how these imposed structures and traditions affect people's opinions of, and interactions with, one another.
6. Nayir muses about the confession he's just obtained from Muhammad: Nouf was planning to abandon her husband in New York and make a life in America. He thinks, "She had died in the desert, but her running to America would have been another kind of death." What does he mean? What is it that disturbs him most about Nouf's secret plans?
7. Katya takes issue with Nayir's belief that Nouf "had everything," arguing that Nouf only "had everything her father let her have." What is the difference? Do you see Nouf as spoiled and ungrateful, as Nayir seems to, or do you sympathize with her desperation, as Katya does?
8. Compare the relationships between Muhammad and Nouf and Ahmad and Katya. Do you agree with Nayir, that Muhammad failed to protect Nouf because he was too busy spoiling her, probably out of his own secret desire for her?
9. Do you think Katya would ever have assimilated into the Shrawi household? What does Othman's behavior in the coatroom indicate to Katya? Why do you think she bursts into tears after leaving?
10. Discuss how Nayir's stereotypical "knowledge" of women limited his theories to possible motives a man would have for kidnapping or killing Nouf. Did you suspect she might have been killed for other reasons, or by a woman? Why or why not?
11. How does the author comment on certain aspects of conservative Islam, such as the Saudi religious police and rules restricting women? Do you feel that you know her opinion by the end of the novel? If so, what is it? If not, why not?

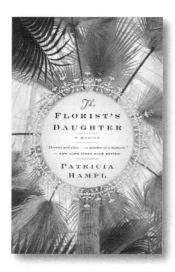

THE FLORIST'S DAUGHTER

AUTHOR: *Patricia Hampl*

PUBLISHER: Mariner Books, 2009

WEBSITE: www.hmhbooks.com
www.patriciahampl.com

AVAILABLE IN:
Trade Paperback, 240 pages, $13.95
ISBN: 978-0-156-03403-6

SUBJECT: Biography/Women's Lives/
Family (Memoir)

"A memoir for memoirists to admire—with language that pierces."
—*Kirkus Reviews*

"With her enchanting prose and transcendent vision, she is indeed a florist's daughter—a purveyor of beauty—as well as a careful, tablet-wielding investigator, ever contemplative, measured and patient in her charge."—*Publishers Weekly*

SUMMARY: During the long farewell of her mother's dying, Patricia Hampl revisits her Midwestern girlhood. Daughter of a debonair Czech father, whose floral work gave him entry into St. Paul society, and a distrustful Irishwoman with an uncanny ability to tell a tale, Hampl remained, primarily and passionately, a daughter well into adulthood. She traces the arc of faithfulness and struggle that comes with that role from the postwar years past the turbulent sixties. *The Florist's Daughter* is a tribute to the ardor of supposedly ordinary people. Its concerns reach beyond a single life to achieve a historic testament to midcentury middle America. At the heart of this book is the humble passion of people who struggled out of the Depression into a better chance, not only for themselves but for the common good. Widely recognized as one of our most masterful memoirists, Patricia Hampl has written her most intimate, yet most universal, work to date.

ABOUT THE AUTHOR: **Patricia Hampl** is the author of four memoirs—*A Romantic Education, Virgin Time, I Could Tell You Stories,* and *Blue Arabesque*—and two collections of poetry. She lives in St. Paul, Minnesota.

1. In the opening of *The Florist's Daughter*, Hampl weaves scenes of the past with images of the long good-bye she shares with her aged mother. How do these opening scenes affect you? Why is this storytelling style so powerful?

2. What were the most significant values that Hampl's parents tried to impart to her? Which of their values had a lasting impact? Which ones became outdated?

3. How would you characterize the author's relationship with her brother? In what ways are their personalities different? What distinctions did the Hampls make between the way sons and daughters should be raised?

4. Discuss the symbolic role of flowers throughout the memoir. What is special about Mr. Hampl's line of work? How was his outlook on life shaped by his being a dealer of roses sent to lovers or luxurious splashes of annuals installed in upper-class flower beds?

5. Though united by Catholicism and a young romance, Hampl's parents overcame differences in culture and temperament to forge a lasting marriage. In what ways did they complete one another?

6. Hampl's father made several unlucky decisions, such as the year he tried to sell expensive imported crèches but (as Leo the Lion predicted) faced a problem with the theft of baby Jesuses. Was Mr. Hampl too much of a romantic to be successful in business, or is financial success a result of other factors?

7. Was Hampl protected from reality? To what extent do most parents try to recapture their own pasts through their children?

8. Discuss the various communities Hampl describes in the St. Paul of her youth. Which groups had the most power? What was the role of religion in shaping a person's standing in the community?

9. What does Hampl discover about her mother when they travel together? What enabled them to see more authentic versions of each other as they grew older? What stood in the way of her mother's dream to become a writer? What stood in the way of Hampl's dream to follow in the path of fellow Minnesotan Scott Fitzgerald and settle on the East Coast?

10. Discuss the experience of becoming the "parent" to aging parents. When Hampl asks the doctor to treat her mother "like a sixteen-year-old who's just crashed on her boyfriend's motorcycle," what is she hoping for? What aspects of her parents' personalities did not fade?

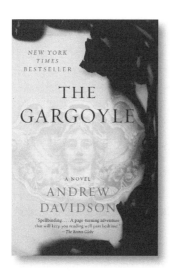

THE GARGOYLE

AUTHOR: *Andrew Davidson*

PUBLISHER: Anchor Books, 2009

WEBSITE: www.thegargoyle.com
www.ReadingGroupCenter.com

AVAILABLE IN:
Trade Paperback, 528 pages, $15.00
ISBN: 978-0-307-38867-4

SUBJECT: Love & Romance/
History/ Relationships (Fiction)

"I was blown away by Andrew Davidson's The Gargoyle. *It reminded me of* Life of Pi, *with its unanswered (and unanswerable) contradictions. A hypnotic, horrifying, astonishing novel that manages, against all odds, to be redemptive."*—**Sara Gruen, author of** *Water for Elephants*

SUMMARY: The Gargoyle is the mesmerizing story of one man's descent into personal hell and his quest for salvation.

On a dark road in the middle of the night, a car plunges into a ravine. The driver survives the crash, but his injuries confine him to a hospital burn unit. There the mysterious Marianne Engel, a sculptress of grotesques, enters his life. She insists they were lovers in medieval Germany, when he was a mercenary and she was a scribe in the monastery of Engelthal. As she spins the story of their past lives together, the man's disbelief falters; soon, even the impossible can no longer be dismissed.

The Gargoyle is an extraordinary debut novel of love that survives the fires of hell and transcends the boundaries of time. Already an international literary sensation, *The Gargoyle* is an *Inferno* for our time. It will have you believing in the impossible.

ABOUT THE AUTHOR: **Andrew Davidson** has worked as a teacher in Japan, where he has lived on and off, and as a writer of English lessons for Japanese Web sites. *The Gargoyle*, the product of seven years' worth of research and composition, is his first book. Davidson lives in Winnipeg, Manitoba.

1. *The Gargoyle* begins with arguably one of the most stunning opening scenes in contemporary literature. How was the author able to make horrifying details alluring? What was your initial reaction to these images?
2. How were you affected by the narrator's voice and his ability to address you in an intimate, direct monologue? How did his storytelling style compare to Marianne's?
3. Arrows form a recurring symbol throughout the novel. What are their various uses as tools of war and of love? What makes them ideal for Marianne's stories?
4. What medical aspects of the narrator's treatment surprised you the most? Did his gruesome journey change the way you feel about your own body?
5. How did Marianne's experience of God evolve and mature throughout her life? How do you personally reconcile the concept of a loving God and the reality of human suffering?
6. Marianne uses her body as a canvas. What messages does it convey? How does the narrator "read" bodies before his accident, both in front of the camera and while picking up less-dazzling strangers?
7. Discuss the role of ghosts and memory in *The Gargoyle*. In what ways does the past repeat itself? How are the characters shaped by past circumstances? When are their painful cycles to be broken?
8. What does Marianne's copy of *The Inferno* indicate about the value of books beyond their content? In what way can a book also be an art object, or an artifact of history?
9. Eventually, Nan reveals her own burn scars. What motivates the novel's healers—including Nan, Marianne, Sayuri, and Gregor? Whom does the narrator heal?
10. Discuss the role of money throughout *The Gargoyle*. What kept Jack honest? What did it mean for Marianne, a woman, to have far more money than the men in her life, both in the 14th century and in the contemporary storyline?
11. How did you interpret the narrator's own Dante-esque tour, described in Chapter Twenty-nine? Was he hallucinating, in the throes of withdrawal while he kicked the bitchsnake of morphine, or did he journey to an underworld? Or both? Was Marianne a mere mortal?
12. An old adage, evidenced particularly in Shakespeare's works, states that a comedy ends with a marriage, while a tragedy ends with a death. Given that *The Gargoyle* ends with both a marriage and a death, what does it say about the work?

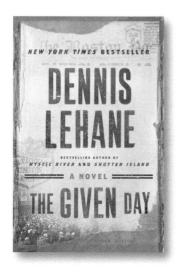

THE GIVEN DAY

AUTHOR: *Dennis Lehane*

PUBLISHER: Harper Perennial, 2009

WEBSITE: www.harperperennial.com
www.dennislehanebooks.com

AVAILABLE IN:
Trade Paperback, 720 pages, $15.99
ISBN: 978-0-380-73187-9

SUBJECT: American History/Family/
Social Issues (Fiction)

"Gut-wrenching force. . . . A majestic, fiery epic. . . . The Given Day is a huge, impassioned, intensively researched book that brings history alive."—The New York Times

"The Given Day is a vast historical novel. . . . Spectacular details. . . . Finely thought-out. . . . Many stunningly managed scenes."—The Boston Globe

SUMMARY: Set in Boston at the end of World War I, *The Given Day* tells the story of two families—one black, one white—swept up in a maelstrom of revolutionaries and anarchists, immigrants and ward bosses, Brahmins and ordinary citizens, all engaged in a battle for survival and power. Beat cop Danny Coughlin, the son of one of the city's most beloved and powerful police captains, joins a burgeoning union movement and the hunt for violent radicals. Luther Laurence, on the run after a deadly confrontation with a crime boss in Tulsa, works for the Coughlin family and tries desperately to find his way home to his pregnant wife. Here, too, are some of the most influential figures of the era—Babe Ruth; Eugene O'Neill; governor Calvin Coolidge; and an ambitious young Department of Justice lawyer named John Hoover. The characters gradually find family in one another and, together, ride a rising storm of hardship, deprivation, and hope that will change all their lives.

ABOUT THE AUTHOR: **Dennis Lehane** has written eight novels, *A Drink Before the War; Darkness, Take My Hand; Sacred; Gone, Baby, Gone; Prayers for Rain; Mystic River; Shutter Island;* and *The Given Day* as well as *Coronado*, a collection of short stories. Lehane lives in the Boston, Massachusetts area.

1. *The Given Day* transports readers to 1918 Boston and touches on the lives of two families—one black, one white—as they are swept up in the maelstrom of history. How are their experiences similar? How are they different?

2. Dennis Lehane writes *The Given Day* from the perspectives of two very different men. What brings Luther Laurence and Danny Coughlin together? Does their friendship ring true?

3. One of the themes of the book is the notion of family—both the blood kind and the kind a person willingly creates on his own. How are these ideas of family manifested? Do you see one as being more important than the other? Can a person belong to two kinds of family at the same time?

4. *The Given Day* centers on the Boston Police Strike of 1919 at a time when fiercely held convictions about work and freedom underwent enormous change at great cost to human life and relationships. Nearly a century later, what is the role of unions in America today? How do the working conditions for Luther and Danny compare to contemporary conditions? Do you think unions are necessary today?

5. How do the themes in the book—race, politics, class, family, immigration, nepotism, corruption—reflect issues facing America today?

6. Injustice is another theme that Lehane explores in the novel. How does injustice manifest itself in democratic societies? Can it be redressed? If so, how?

7. What role does Babe Ruth play in the narrative? What did the introduction of his character add to your understanding of the novel's main themes?

8. Who do you think is the most sympathetic character in the story? Why?

9. What role does Danny play in each character's development? How do they, in turn, influence him?

10. Talk about the relationship of Danny and his father. How are they alike? How are they different? How do their similarities and differences shape their relationship?

11. What role do women play in the novel? How do they impact the men?

12. Consider your own life experiences. How would you have fared in the America of a century ago? If Danny and Luther were transported to 21st-century America, what might they think of our world?

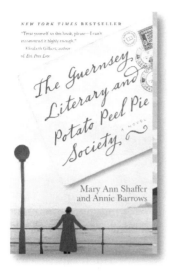

THE GUERNSEY LITERARY AND POTATO PEEL PIE SOCIETY

AUTHORS: **Mary Ann Shaffer**
Annie Barrows

PUBLISHER: Dial Press Trade Paperback, 2009

WEBSITE: www.guernseyliterary.com

AVAILABLE IN:
Trade Paperback, 304 pages, $14.00
ISBN: 978-0-385-34100-4

SUBJECT: Relationships/Identity/History (Fiction)

"I can't remember the last time I discovered a novel as smart and delightful as this one, a world so vivid that I kept forgetting this was a work of fiction populated with characters so utterly wonderful that I kept forgetting they weren't my actual friends and neighbors. Treat yourself to this book please—I can't recommend it highly enough."—**Elizabeth Gilbert, author of** *Eat, Pray, Love*

SUMMARY: Celebrating literature, love, and the power of the human spirit, *The Guernsey Literary and Potato Peel Pie Society* is the story of an English author living in the shadow of World War II—and embarking on a writing project that will dramatically change her life. Unfolding in a series of letters, this enchanting novel introduces readers to the indomitable Juliet Ashton. She begins a correspondence, responding to a man who found her name on the flyleaf of a cherished secondhand book. His name is Dawsey Adams, a native resident of Guernsey, one of the Channel Islands recently liberated from Nazi occupation. Soon Juliet is drawn into Dawsey's remarkable circle of friends, courageous men and women who formed the Guernsey Literary and Potato Peel Pie Society as a cover to protect them from the Germans. With their appetite for good books, and their determination to honor the island's haunting recent history, this is a community that opens Juliet's heart and mind in ways she could never have imagined.

ABOUT THE AUTHORS: **Mary Ann Shaffer** worked as an editor, a librarian, and in bookshops. *The Guernsey Literary and Potato Peel Pie Society* was her first novel. Her niece, **Annie Barrows**, is the author of the children's series Ivy and Bean, as well as *The Magic Half*.

1. What was it like to read a novel composed entirely of letters? What do letters offer that no other form of writing (not even emails) can convey?
2. What makes Sidney and Sophie ideal friends for Juliet? What common ground do they share? Who has been a similar advocate in your life?
3. Dawsey first wrote to Juliet because books, on Charles Lamb or otherwise, were so difficult to obtain on Guernsey in the aftermath of the war. What differences did you note between bookselling in the novel and bookselling in your world? What makes book lovers unique, across all generations?
4. What were your first impressions of Dawsey? How was he different from the other men Juliet had known?
5. Discuss the poets, novelists, biographers, and other writers who capture the hearts of the members of the Guernsey Literary and Potato Peel Pie Society. Whose lives were changed the most by membership in the society?
6. Juliet occasionally receives mean-spirited correspondence from strangers, accusing both Elizabeth and Juliet of being immoral. What accounts for their judgmental ways?
7. In what ways were Juliet and Elizabeth kindred spirits? What did Elizabeth's spontaneous invention of the society, as well as her brave final act, say about her approach to life?
8. Numerous Guernsey residents give Juliet access to their private memories of the occupation. Which voices were most memorable for you? What was the effect of reading a variety of responses to a shared tragedy?
9. Kit and Juliet complete each other in many ways. What did they need from each other? What qualities make Juliet an unconventional, excellent mother?
10. How did Remy's presence enhance the lives of those on Guernsey? Through her survival, what recollections, hopes, and lessons also survived?
11. What historical facts about life in England during World War II were you especially surprised to discover? What traits, such as remarkable stamina, are captured in a detail such as potato peel pie? In what ways does fiction provide a means for more fully understanding a non-fiction truth?
12. Which of the members of the Society is your favorite? Whose literary opinions are most like your own?
13. Do you agree with Isola that "reading good books ruins you for enjoying bad ones"?

HEART AND SOUL

AUTHOR: *Maeve Binchy*

PUBLISHER: Anchor Books, February 2010

WEBSITE: www.ReadingGroupCenter.com
www.maevebinchy.com

AVAILABLE IN:
Trade Paperback, 576 pages, $7.99
ISBN: 978-0-307-27842-5

SUBJECT: Family/Humor/Relationships
(Fiction)

"A modern day women's writer in the Jane Austen sense."
—**Lauren Daley,** *The Standard-Times*

"Another delightful Binchyesque amalgamation of intersecting lives . . . the collective, charming effect of these story lines suggests that individuals are more connected than they might think."—***Publishers Weekly***

SUMMARY: With the insight, humor, and compassion we have come to expect from her, Maeve Binchy tells a story of family, friends, patients, and staff who are part of a heart clinic in a community caught between the old and the new Ireland.

Dr. Clara Casey has been offered the thankless job of establishing the underfunded clinic and agrees to take it on for a year. She has plenty on her plate already—two difficult adult daughters and the unwanted attentions of her ex-husband—but she assembles a wonderfully diverse staff devoted to helping their demanding, often difficult patients. Before long the clinic is established as an essential part of the community, and Clara must decide whether or not to leave a place where lives are saved, courage is rewarded, and humor and optimism triumph over greed and self-pity.

Heart and Soul is Maeve Binchy at her storytelling best.

ABOUT THE AUTHOR: **Maeve Binchy** is the author of numerous best-selling books, including her most recent novel, *Whitethorn Woods*, in addition to *Night of Rain and Stars*, *Quentins*, *Scarlet Feather*, *Circle of Friends*, and *Tara Road*, which was an Oprah's Book Club selection. She and her husband, Gordon Snell, live in Dalkey, Ireland, and London.

1. Have you read any of Maeve Binchy's other books? If you've encountered any of these characters before, how did this new novel deepen your understanding of them? If you haven't, which characters would you like to spend more time with?

2. It's clear what the "heart" of the title refers to, but who—or what—is the "soul"?

3. The heart clinic is the embodiment of a new idea that advocates teaching people about their health without having to go to a hospital or to a doctor who may not have much time to spend with an individual patient. Why do you think the heart clinic is a good idea? Is there such a thing in your town or neighborhood?

4. There are many different mothers in the novel. Who does Binchy portray as a good mother? In what ways? Which mother would you most like to have as your own?

5. How are Binchy's mother-daughter relationships different from her mother-son ones?

6. What role does the "new Ireland" play in *Heart and Soul*? Is Quentins part of the new Ireland and if so how? What other aspects of this novel reflect the new Ireland?

7. Discuss the bigotry Ania faces, especially by Rosemary. In what ways is the treatment of new immigrants different in Ireland than it is in this country?

8. Several of the women have had relationships with abusive and entirely untrustworthy men. How does their prior history affect their current romances? Are these relationships healthier than the previous ones because of the men involved, or have the women themselves changed?

9. Was Eileen Edwards genuinely delusional, or do you think she had another reason for blackmailing Father Flynn? What did you think of Johnny's solution to Father Flynn's problem? Who benefited the most from the resolution?

10. Twice in the novel, characters state, "We always regret what we *don't* do, rarely what we *do* do." Who follows this code to the greatest advantage? Is there anyone who should apply it but doesn't?

11. Who is the most contented character in the novel? The most disappointed? What role does money play in their happiness?

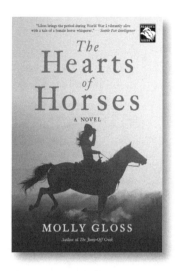

THE HEARTS OF HORSES

AUTHOR: *Molly Gloss*

PUBLISHER: Mariner Books, 2008

WEBSITE: www.hmhbooks.com
www.mollygloss.com

AVAILABLE IN:
Trade Paperback, 304 pages, $13.95
ISBN: 978-0-547-08575-3

SUBJECT: Women's Lives/Relationships/
Personal Triumph (Fiction)

"An acutely observed, often lyrical portrayal . . . has as much to say about people as about horses."—**Kirkus Reviews**

"Not just a horse story or a tale of the West, Gloss's moving novel . . . is a story not soon forgotten."—**Bookpage**

SUMMARY: In the winter of 1917, nineteen-year-old Martha Lessen saddles her horses and heads for a remote county in eastern Oregon, looking for work "gentling" wild horses. She chances on a rancher, George Bliss, who is willing to hire her on. Many of his regular hands are off fighting the war, and he glimpses, beneath her showy rodeo garb, a shy but strong-willed girl with a serious knowledge of horses.

So begins the irresistible tale of a young but determined woman trying to make a go of it in a man's world. Over the course of several long, hard winter months, many of the townsfolk witness Martha talking in low, sweet tones to horses believed beyond repair—and getting miraculous, almost immediate results. Ultimately, her gifts will earn her a place of respect in the community.

ABOUT THE AUTHOR: **Molly Gloss** is the author of *Wild Life*, winner of the James Tiptree Award; *The Jump-Off Creek*, a finalist for the PEN/Faulkner Award; and *The Dazzle of Day*, a *New York Times* Notable Book. She lives in Portland, Oregon.

1. What are Martha's methods for breaking horses? How do they differ from most other people? What challenges does Martha face as a female broncobuster and how does she overcome them?
2. Why do so many characters take notice of Martha's outfit, dressing "like she's headed off to a rodeo"?
3. Many of the characters in the novel come across as very lonely. What makes Elwha County such a lonely place? How is Martha's loneliness different from Dorothy's?
4. Kent Haruf said of Molly Gloss and *The Hearts of Horses*: "She's given us . . . a great deal of lore about the gentling of horses—a gentling that suggests both a practical fact and an enduring metaphor." Explore the gentling of horses as a metaphor. What's the secret to Martha's horse whispering? How does Martha's gift with horses reflect her character?
5. Because of the war, many of the German families in Elwha County are mistreated, there are grand displays of patriotism, and many sacrifices are made for the greater good. How are these consequences of war similar to or different from those which occurred during wars the U.S. has fought in since WWI? Do you see reflections of the current war in Iraq?
6. Martha judges people by how they treat their horses. The Thiedes notice that she had "evidently made up her mind that people who treated horses decently must be decent people." How do you form your opinion of people? What is your moral compass?
7. Martha is responsible for getting Al Logerwell fired for beating horses. What are the repercussions of Martha's actions? Later, she repeats a comment she heard from the Woodruff sisters when she says, "Well, there are plenty of men who will beat a horse. But they'd just better not do it in front of me is all." What is the significance of this statement?
8. Why does Louise Bliss avoid all news of the war? Why does the library she attempts to open through the Elwha Valley Literary Society become such a sensitive issue?
9. What does Martha tell Henry she wants out of a marriage and how is he able to give these things to her? What makes Henry different from most men Martha has known?
10. How is this book about the "hearts of horses"? Which horses are characters and what are their roles? What else might the title be referring to?
11. In the last paragraph of the book, Martha tells her granddaughter, "I guess we brought about the end of our cowboy dreams ourselves." What does she mean by this? Do you agree with her?

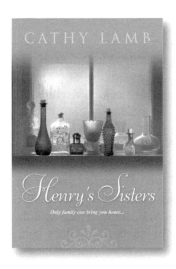

HENRY'S SISTERS

AUTHOR: *Cathy Lamb*

PUBLISHER: Kensington Books, 2009

WEBSITE: www.cathylamb.net
www.kensingtonbooks.com

AVAILABLE IN:
Trade Paperback, 352 pages, $15.00
ISBN: 978-0-7582-2954-0

SUBJECT: Family/Women's Lives/Identity
(Fiction)

"Lamb delivers grace, humor, and forgiveness along with a litany of family trauma . . . this finely pitched family melodrama is balanced with enough gallows of humor and idiosyncratic characters to make it positively irresistible."—Publishers Weekly

SUMMARY: Cathy Lamb, the acclaimed author of *Julia's Chocolates* and *The Last Time I Was Me*, delivers her most heartwarming novel to date as three sisters reunite during a family crisis. Ever since the Bommarito sisters were little girls, their mother, River, has written them a letter on pink paper when she has something especially important to impart. And this time, the message is urgent and impossible to ignore—River requires open-heart surgery, and Isabelle and her sisters are needed at home to run the family bakery and take care of their brother and ailing grandmother. But going home again has a way of forcing open the secrets and hurts that the Bommaritos would rather keep tightly closed—Isabelle's fleeting and too-frequent relationships, Janie's obsessive compulsive disorder, and Cecilia's self-destructive streak and grief over her husband's death. Isabelle and her sisters begin to find answers to questions they never knew existed, unexpected ways to salve the wounds of their childhoods, and the courage to grasp surprising new chances at happiness. *Henry's Sisters* is a novel about family and forgiveness, about mothers and daughters, and about gaining the wisdom to look ahead while still holding tight to everything that matters most.

ABOUT THE AUTHOR: **Cathy Lamb**, the author of *Julia's Chocolates, The Last Time I Was Me*, and *Henry's Sisters*, lives in Oregon. She is married with three children.

1. Of the three sisters, whom do you relate to the most? With whom would you most likely be friends? If you had to change places with one of the sisters for a month, which one would you trade places with? What would you do to change their lives in that month, if anything?
2. How did Isabelle change from the beginning of the book to the end? Cecilia? Janie? What do you think is in the future for each of the sisters?
3. River made many difficult decisions when the sisters and Henry were growing up. Was River backed into a corner, or were there other decisions she could have made? What would you have done? Is it judgmental to say that we would not have made the same decisions as she did if we were in her shoes?
4. Do you agree with Carl's decision to stay away from the family? Would you have been able to forgive your husband if he left for thirty years, given the same circumstances, as River did? Would you have been able to forgive your father for an absence of that length?
5. Did Henry have a happy life? What could all of us learn from Henry?
6. What role did Father Mike play in this book? How did his words help Isabelle recover from who she used to be? Would you describe Isabelle as religious?
7. Velvet Eddow said, "Men are easily baffled, though, darlin', don't ever forget that. Their brains think like porn. That's the only way I can describe it, darlin', like porn. . . . One part of their brain thinks, the other part is holding a breast in his hand, at all times." True? Not true?
8. Cecilia and Isabelle had an intense emotional/physical twin connection to each other. Do you believe that these types of connections exist between twins, siblings, or family members? If so, how does this happen? Did this connection enhance the story?
9. The sisters, and Henry, all suffered from their childhood. In the end, did it make them stronger? More compassionate? Or was the fallout so extreme for all of them that they'll never fully recover? How did their childhoods affect their future careers?
10. How did Henry hold the family together? Do you agree with the author's decision to have Henry die by the end of the book? Was there any other ending that would have worked?
11. Describe the sisters' relationships to one another. Is the Bommarito family a functioning or a nonfunctioning family? Is your family like this to some extent?

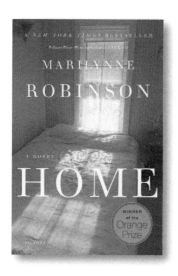

HOME

AUTHOR: *Marilynne Robinson*

PUBLISHER: Picador USA, 2009

WEBSITE: us.macmillan.com/home

AVAILABLE IN:
Trade Paperback, 336 pages, $14.00
ISBN: 978-0-312-42854-9

SUBJECT: Family/Faith/Relationships
(Fiction)

2009 Winner of the Orange Prize

"Remarkable . . . an even stronger accomplishment than Gilead.*"*—**Claire Messud,** *The New York Review of Books*

"Home begins simply, eschewing obvious verbal fineness, and slowly grows in luxury—its last fifty pages are magnificently moving. . . . Powerful." —**James Wood,** *The New Yorker*

SUMMARY: Hailed as "incandescent," "magnificent," and "a literary miracle" (*Entertainment Weekly*), hundreds of thousands of readers were enthralled by Marilynne Robinson's *Gilead*. Now Robinson returns with a brilliantly imagined retelling of the prodigal son parable, set at the same moment and in the same Iowa town as Gilead. The Reverend Boughton's hell-raising son, Jack, has come home after twenty years away. Artful and devious in his youth, now an alcoholic carrying two decade's worth of secrets, he is perpetually at odds with his traditionalist father, though he remains his most beloved child. As Jack tries to make peace with his father, he begins to forge an intense bond with his sister Glory, herself returning home with a broken heart and turbulent past. *Home* is a luminous and healing book about families, family secrets, and faith from one of America's most beloved and acclaimed authors.

ABOUT THE AUTHOR: **Marilynne Robinson** is the author of the novels *Gilead, Housekeeping*, and two books of nonfiction, *Mother Country* and *The Death of Adam*. She teaches at the University of Iowa Writers' Workshop.

1. What does "home" mean to Robert Boughton and his children? What does the Boughton house signify to his family? With whom do they feel most at home?

2. How is the Boughton household affected by the presence of a television set? How does this reflect a shift that took place in many American households in the 1950s? Were you surprised by Robert's comments about African Americans, and by his reaction to the televised race riots?

3. Why do you think Robert loves Jack best, despite Jack's shortcomings? What is your understanding of Jack's wayward behavior? How would you have responded to his theological questions regarding redemption?

4. Discuss the friendship between John Ames and Robert Boughton. What has sustained it for so many years? How did they nurture each other's intellectual lives, approaching life from Congregationalist and Presbyterian perspectives?

5. What did Glory's mother teach her about the role of women? How was the Boughton family affected by the death of its matriarch?

6. How do the Boughtons view prosperity and charity? What is reflected in the way Glory handles the household finances, with leftover money stored in the piano bench?

7. How do the themes of deception and integrity play out in the novel? Are all of the characters honest with themselves? Which secrets, in the novel and in life, are justified?

8. How are Glory, Jack, and Robert affected by Teddy's visit? What accounts for the "anxiety, and relief, and resentment" Glory feels regarding Teddy's arrival?

9. Discuss Ames's provocative sermon, which Jack paraphrases as a discussion of "the disgraceful abandonment of children by their fathers" based on the narrative of Hagar and Ishmael. To what degree are parents responsible for the actions of their children, and vice versa?

10. How did you react to Della's arrival? What legacy and memories will define her son? What common ground did Jack and Della share, fostering love?

11. In terms of religion, what beliefs do Glory, Jack, and Robert agree upon? What do they seek to know about God and the nature of humanity?

12. What are the similarities and differences between the Ames and Boughton households?

13. Discuss the homecomings that have made a significant impact on your life. How much forgiveness has been necessary across the generations in your family?

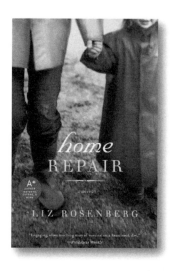

HOME REPAIR

AUTHOR: *Liz Rosenberg*

PUBLISHER: Avon A, 2009

WEBSITE: www.avonbooks.com

AVAILABLE IN:
Trade Paperback, 352 pages, $13.99
ISBN: 978-0-061-73456-4

SUBJECT: Family/Love & Romance/
Personal Discovery (Fiction)

SUMMARY: Can lighting really strike twice? Just ask Eve, whose husband walks out on her in the middle of a garage sale. Now Eve is left to contend with two growing children, and an elderly, well-meaning and stubborn mother who rushes in to "help." Filled with an equal measure of hilarity and heartbreak (including some "heartbreak diet" tips along the way).

A poignant, lovely, funny, and ultimately uplifting story of love, family, and survival, Liz Rosenberg's *Home Repair* is an unforgettable introduction to a lyrical, wise, and wonderfully vibrant new literary voice.

ABOUT THE AUTHOR: **Liz Rosenberg** is the author of *Little Gathering Poems, Earth-Shattering Poems, Invisible Ladder*, and *On Christmas Eve*. She has received numerous recognitions including an IRA-CBC Children's Choice and has been featured on Reading Rainbow. She lives in Binghamton, New York.

1. Why do you think this book is called *Home Repair*? Who and what is broken in this novel, and how does it get repaired?

2. Eve initially responds to her situation by going on "The Heartbreak Diet" and dressing out of her hamper. Does this ring true to you? How have you, or the people or other literary characters you've known, reacted to heartbreak?

3. They say that a tragedy ends with a death, and a comedy ends with a marriage. Since *Home Repair* has some of each, do you think this is more of a tragic or a comic novel?

4. In some ways, *Home Repair* is about change. What are some of the notable changes in this novel?

5. There are many minor characters all through the novel: Mia; Jonah; Clem; Devin; Maxine Schwartz etc. How do you feel they strengthen or distract from the novel?

6. The last chapter of the book has a surprise element. What did you think was going to happen? What did you want to happen?

7. What is the role of family in the novel? What is the role of friendship?

8. Marcus goes through some tough experiences in this novel. Are they believable, and do you think teenagers really have to face challenges like this?

9. What is the role of Rec Park in this book? Does it represent anything beyond itself?

10. There is a big, messy Thanksgiving dinner in the middle of this book. Why do you think the author chose Thanksgiving for this scene? What is the meaning of this scene for the rest of the book?

11. Marcus challenges the Senator to a debate. Should young people be more or less involved in politics? How can they be involved effectively?

12. Who would you say is the most heroic character in this novel, and why?

13. Charlotte says to her daughter, "We're all going to someday say good-bye, little girl. We're all going to have to cry." Do you believe this is true? If you had to say one thing to someone about loss, what would it be?

14. In the chapter called "On the Diet" Eve realizes "she simply didn't have any time or space to weep in. She'd have to give it up and move on." In what other ways is she constrained? What are some of the ways people make space for themselves in this novel? How does the idea of an open space come to play in the book?

15. What is the meaning and purpose of Van Gogh in this book? Olivia says that "Art can save lives…. Van Gogh's failures teach us never to give up hope." What do you think the role of art should be?

HOPE'S BOY

AUTHOR: *Andrew Bridge*

PUBLISHER: Hyperion Books, 2009

WEBSITE: www.hyperionbooks.com

AVAILABLE IN:
Trade Paperback, $14.95
ISBN: 9781401309749

SUBJECT: Family/Relationships/Identity
(Memoir)

"Bridge, a Harvard Law School graduate who has devoted his career to children's rights, has provided remarkable insights into a dark corner of American society."—Publishers Weekly

"Critics Choice . . . Shocking, inspiring, unforgettable."—People magazine

"In luminous prose and heartwrenching detail, Andrew Bridge reminds us to honor the power of love in our fractured world."—**Caroline Kennedy**

SUMMARY: Trapped in desperate poverty and confronted with unthinkable tragedies, all Andrew ever wanted was to be with his mom. But as her mental health steadily declined, and with no one else left to care for him, authorities arrived and tore Andrew from his screaming mother's arms. He was only seven years old. Hope was institutionalized, and Andrew was placed in what would be his devastating reality for the next eleven years— foster care. After surviving one of our country's most notorious children's facilities, Andrew was thrust into a savagely loveless foster family that refused to accept him as one of their own. Deprived of the nurturing he needed, Andrew clung to academics and the kindness of teachers. Andrew has dedicated his life's work to helping children living in poverty and in the foster care system. He defied the staggering odds set against him, and here in this heart-wrenching, brutally honest, and inspirational memoir, he reveals who Hope's boy really is.

ABOUT THE AUTHOR: Formerly the CEO/General Counsel of The Alliance for Children's Rights, **Andrew Bridge** lives in New York City. He remains a dedicated and vocal advocate for children in foster care.

1. Given her circumstances, do you think that Hope did as much as she could? Should she have done more? Were there qualities that you liked about her?

2. Have you ever seen a situation of a young mother like Hope clearly struggling to keep and care for her child? What was your own response to seeing the situation?

3. Andy's foster mother, Mrs. Leonard, was a child survivor of a concentration camp. How much of that experience do you think influenced her parenting, as a mother and foster mother?

4. Should foster parents be regarded more like paid employees or like charitable volunteers? Should we expect foster parents to put up with the same level of behavior that they would from their own children?

5. If you were a foster parent, what would you have told Andy to say when other children or classmates asked him about his past or his parents? Would it be right to tell him to lie to protect himself?

6. Do Andy and the other foster children he describes seem typical of what you know of foster children today?

7. Did you have any similar relationships with your childhood teachers, as Andy did?

8. Given the importance of Andy's teachers and schools, do you think that he would have been better off moved to a different home and therefore a different school?

9. Would you consider adopting a foster child? Why or why not?

10. What do you think are the greatest problems confronting impoverished families today? Should officials have done more to keep Hope and Andy together or to allow them to continue to have a relationship while he was in foster care?

11. What are your thoughts on fostering, adopting, or mentoring a child in state care? What special skills do you possess that might be worth sharing with a child or family in need?

12. Did *Hope's Boy* change your view of what it is like to grow up in foster care? Of all the stories in *Hope's Boy*, what scenes were the most memorable, the most painful, the most inspiring?

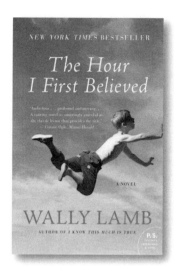

THE HOUR I FIRST BELIEVED

AUTHOR: **Wally Lamb**

PUBLISHER: Harper Perennial, 2009

WEBSITE: www.harperperennial.com

AVAILABLE IN:
Trade Paperback, 768 pages, $15.99
ISBN: 978-0-060-98843-2

SUBJECT: Family/Faith/Social Issues
(Fiction)

"[Lamb] knows just how to let the details of a tragedy unfold without decoration or commentary. He's a master at the kind of direct, unadorned narrative that brings these events alive in all their visceral power. . . . wholly sympathetic, deeply moving."—**Ron Charles, Washington Post Book World**

SUMMARY: In *The Hour I First Believed*, Lamb travels well beyond his earlier work and embodies in his fiction myth, psychology, family history stretching back many generations, and the questions of faith that lie at the heart of everyday life. When high school teacher Caelum Quirk and his wife, Maureen, move to Littleton, Colorado, they both get jobs at Columbine High School. In April 1999, Caelum returns home to Three Rivers, Connecticut, to be with his aunt who has just had a stroke. But Maureen finds herself in the school library at Columbine, cowering in a cabinet and expecting to be killed, as two students go on a murderous rampage. Miraculously she survives. Caelum and Maureen flee Colorado and return to an illusion of safety in Three Rivers. But the effects of chaos are not so easily put right, and further tragedy ensues. As Caelum grapples with unexpected and confounding revelations from the past, he also struggles to fashion a future out of the ashes of tragedy. His personal quest for meaning and faith becomes a mythic journey that is at the same time quintessentially contemporary—and American.

ABOUT THE AUTHOR: **Wally Lamb** wrote the number one *New York Times* bestsellers *She's Come Undone* and *I Know This Much Is True*. Lamb still contributes time as a volunteer facilitator at the York Correctional Institution. He lives in Connecticut with his wife, Christine.

1. *The Hour I First Believed* deals with many themes: violence, family, the quest for meaning and connection, faith, and the power of chaos to change our lives. These themes are stitched together by two opposing emotional states—despair and hope. How are these two oppositional states intertwined in the story? How are they demonstrated in the story? Use any of the character's lives as an example.

2. Do you believe that out of chaos—tragedy—comes understanding and hope? Is this always the case?

3. Can perpetrators of chaos be victims themselves? Which, if any of the characters, demonstrate this? If you answer no, why not?

4. One of the major themes of the book is violence. Can violence ever be justified? Is it sometimes necessary? Is war always immoral?

5. How does Caelum and Maureen's relationship evolve from the beginning of the story to its conclusion? Why did they stay together?

6. Why does Velvet call Maureen Mom? Why do you think they were able to form such a powerful bond? What did each give to the other?

7. Do you think Caelum could have found his hour of belief without the events he experienced?

8. What does the title *The Hour I First Believed* mean to you? Have you had a moment of belief or witnessed it in another's life?

9. Caelum's aunt, Lolly, lived by the philosophy of the sign that hung behind her desk at the prison: "A woman who surrenders her freedom need not surrender her dignity." What did that mean to Lolly? What does that mean to you? Did Maureen find freedom in her imprisonment?

10. The novel recalls the debate of nature versus nurture. How much are we the sum of our families? How much can we change?

11. Fate and free will also play a role throughout the novel. How are the two connected? How are fate and free will related to nature and nurture?

12. Do you believe in rehabilitation? Do you think kindness is important even when it comes to criminals? Why or why not?

13. Have your views of crime, prison, and criminals changed in any way from your reading of the novel?

14. Is it fair or unfair to blend fiction and nonfiction? Was it fair of Lamb to draw on the actual Columbine tragedy, or should he have created a fictional school shooting incident?

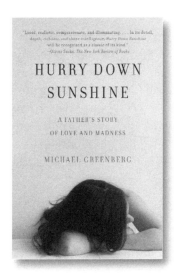

HURRY DOWN SUNSHINE

AUTHOR: *Michael Greenberg*

PUBLISHER: Vintage Books, 2009

WEBSITE: www.ReadingGroupCenter.com

AVAILABLE IN:
Trade Paperback, 256 pages, $14.95
ISBN: 978-0-307-47354-7

SUBJECT: Biography/Family/
Personal Challenges (Memoir)

"Lucid, realistic, compassionate, and illuminating. . . . In its detail, depth, richness and sheer intelligence, Hurry Down Sunshine *will be recognized as a classic of its kind."*—**Oliver Sacks**, *The New York Review of Books*

SUMMARY: *Hurry Down Sunshine* is an extraordinary family story and a memoir of exceptional power. In it, Michael Greenberg recounts in vivid detail the remarkable summer when, at the age of fifteen, his daughter was struck mad. It begins with Sally's sudden visionary crack-up on the streets of Greenwich Village, and continues, among other places, in the out-of-time world of a Manhattan psychiatric ward during the city's most sweltering months. It is a tale of a family broken open, then painstakingly, movingly stitched together again.

Among Greenberg's unforgettable cast of characters are an unconventional psychiatrist, an Orthodox Jewish patient, a manic Classics professor, a movie producer, and a landlord with literary aspirations. Unsentimental, nuanced, and deeply humane, *Hurry Down Sunshine* is essential reading in the literature of affliction alongside classics such as *Girl, Interrupted* and *An Unquiet Mind*.

ABOUT THE AUTHOR: **Michael Greenberg** is a columnist for the *Times Literary Supplement* (London), where his wide-ranging essays have been appearing since 2003. His fiction, criticism, and travel pieces have been published in such varied places as *O, The Oprah Magazine, Bomb, The Village Voice*, and *The New York Review of Books*. He lives in New York with his wife and son.

1. Why does the author doubt Sally's psychosis? How does each family member deal with the crisis differently, and what do their reactions tell you about them?

2. Consider the author's grief over Sally's illness in relation to his mother's guilt over her troubled son, Steven. In what ways are parental guilt intensified in times of crisis?

3. Before her psychotic episode, Sally refuses to believe Pat's devotion to her is sincere. How does their relationship change as Sally battles to overcome the psychosis? How does Pat's revelation about her close friend after the fight with Michael shed light on her devotion to Sally as a mother?

4. How does the Hasidic family respond to Noah's psychosis? How was it different from Sally's family? Were there any similarities? Why do you think Noah and Sally were drawn to each other?

5. Throughout the story, the author interjects scenes that reflect current events happening in the world. How does Greenberg use these events to give the reader a better understanding of what he is going through?

6. How is the narrator's relationship with his brother, Steven, both a responsibility he enjoys as well as a source of burden for him? Cite examples.

7. Greenberg describes infant Sally, as distinctly fiery: "a thrasher, a gripper, a grasper, a yanker of fingers and ears". In what ways does Sally's madness inform the way the author reflects on her infancy and childhood?

8. In the midst of a crisis, families either pull together or are torn apart. How did Sally's illness change the dynamics between family members?

9. How is psychosis understood and misunderstood in society, and how has this changed over time? If Steven were raised in Sally's generation, do you think he would have turned out differently?

10. Do you feel that Greenberg and Pat and Robin did a good job in caring for Sally during her time of crisis? Would you have responded differently?

11. James Joyce called psychosis "the most elusive disease known to man and unknown to medicine." Do you think metal illness is a medical disease or an extreme aspect of who we are as human beings?

12. Do you think it is possible to separate Sally's behavior while psychotic from her personality and way of being when she is not psychotic or do they seem to be aspects of a single person?

I SEE YOU EVERYWHERE

AUTHOR: *Julia Glass*

PUBLISHER: Anchor Books, 2009

WEBSITE: www.ReadingGroupCenter.com

AVAILABLE IN:
Trade Paperback, 304 pages, $15.00
ISBN: 978-1-400-07577-5

SUBJECT: Family/Relationships/
Women's Lives (Fiction)

"Rich, intricate and alive with emotion. . . . An honest portrait of sister-love and sister-hate—interlocking, brave and forgiving—made whole through art."—The New York Times Book Review

SUMMARY: Julia Glass, the bestselling, National Book Award-winning author of *Three Junes*, returns with a tender, riveting book of two sisters and their complicated relationship.

Louisa Jardine is the older one, the conscientious student, precise and careful: the one who yearns for a good marriage, an artistic career, a family. Clem, the archetypal youngest, is the rebel: committed to her work saving animals, but not to the men who fall for her. In this vivid, heartrending story of what we can and cannot do for those we love, the sisters grow closer as they move further apart. All told with sensual detail and deft characterization, *I See You Everywhere* is a candid story of life and death, companionship and sorrow, and the nature of sisterhood itself.

ABOUT THE AUTHOR: **Julia Glass** is the author of *Three Junes,* which won the National Book Award for Fiction, and *The Whole World Over.* She has received fellowships from the National Endowment for the Arts, the New York Foundation for the Arts, and the Radcliffe Institute for Advanced Study. Her short fiction has won several prizes, including the Tobias Wolff Award and the Pirate's Alley Faulkner Society Medal for the Best Novella. She lives with her family in Massachusetts.

1. *I See You Everywhere* focuses on the relationship of Louisa and Clement Jardine. Describe each sister's character. How are they like and unlike each other—also, like and unlike their parents? What do their attitudes toward work, love, and family have in common? How do they differ?

2. Glass has chosen to tell this story through alternating perspectives and, from both sides, in first person. How does this affect your reading? How do you relate to both sisters and see them differently than perhaps they are able to see each other?

3. How does letter writing create a different relationship between two people than e-mail does? Does a separate sense of Clem as a person emerge in her letters? What does it mean that Clem chooses R.B. as the recipient of her final, most significant letter? Read through that letter again. Do you think it has the impact she intended on those who will see it? Do you think she suspected that R.B. would not keep it to himself? Does the letter change the way you saw and felt about her up to this point in the book?

4. Cooking is meaningful in all of Glass's fiction. What role does it play in this book?

5. Describe the sisters' relationship with their parents. Do you see these bonds echoed in your own life, with your parents or children?

6. Do you agree with Ralph, that Clem "*needed* to be fearless," that her fearlessness was a screen for fear? If so, what do you think she feared so deeply? Why do you think she is able to desire for her sister what she herself avoids—a family, a steady relationship, a certain kind of calm?

7. What role does Louisa's cancer play in the story? Do you think it has any influence on Clem's ultimate, fatal decision? At the end, Louisa acknowledges to Campbell that Clem was ill. Would Clem have agreed?

8. Do Louisa and Clem, despite their insistence on how differently they approach men, share a certain confusion when it comes to sexual and romantic desire? What does "love" mean to each sister?

9. If you've read Glass's first two novels, *Three Junes* and *The Whole World Over*, how do the families in this new story relate to the families she's written about in the past?

10. Do you think others understand Clem well or not at all? How well does she understand herself? Do you think this statement could apply to the other characters as well? Which ones and why?

11. What about love makes Clem feel broken and unable to be whole? After Danny's death, she concludes that "the opposite of happiness isn't unhappiness. . . . It's surrender." What do you think about this idea?

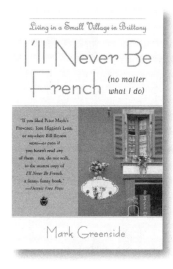

I'LL NEVER BE FRENCH
(no matter what I do)
Living in a Small Village in Brittany

AUTHOR: *Mark Greenside*

PUBLISHER: Free Press, 2009

WEBSITE: www.simonandschuster.com
www.markgreenside.com

AVAILABLE IN:
Trade Paperback, 256 pages, $14.99
ISBN: 978-1-4165-8695-1

SUBJECT: Culture & World Issues/
Relationships/Identity (Memoir)

"One of the nicest of the trillions of books about France."—**Diane Johnson,** author of *L'Affaire, Le Mariage,* and *Le Divorce*

SUMMARY: Tired of Provence in books, cuisine, and tablecloths? Exhausted from your armchair travels to Paris? Despairing of ever finding a place that speaks to you beyond reason? You are ripe for a journey to Brittany, where author Mark Greenside reluctantly travels, eats of the crêpes, and finds a second life.

When Mark Greenside—a native New Yorker living in California, doubting (not-as-trusting-as Thomas), downwardly mobile, political lefty, writer, and lifelong skeptic—is dragged by his girlfriend to a tiny Celtic village in Brittany at the westernmost edge of France, in Finistère, "the end of the world," his life begins to change.

I'll Never Be French (no matter what I do) is a beginning and a homecoming for Greenside, as his father's family emigrated from France. It is a memoir about fitting in, not standing out; being part of something larger, not being separate from it; following, not leading. It explores the joys and adventures of living a double life.

ABOUT THE AUTHOR: **Mark Greenside** is the author of the short story collection *I Saw a Man Hit* His Wife. His stories have also appeared in several magazines, including *The Sun, The Literary Review*, and *Cimarron Review*. Greenside lives in Alameda, California, as well as in Brittany, France, where, he says, he still can't do anything without asking for help.

1. The author often writes about being American. What does it mean to him? What does it mean to you? What differences does he discover between being American and French?
2. The author is a stranger in a foreign land. He has to make do with very rudimentary French. How does he communicate? From his communication skills, what did you discover about how language is learned and created?
3. Who are your most favorite and least favorite characters in the book? Why?
4. What scenes made you laugh the most and what scenes disturbed you the most? Why?
5. How did the author change from the beginning of the book to the end? Is he a different person at the end? If so, how is he different?
6. What does the author learn about himself?
7. The author makes a big distinction between comfort and convenience, and how the French seem to be very good at the former and less good at the latter. Is the distinction significant? What does it tell you about French and American values?
8. Were you surprised by all of the reminders of World Wars I and II? What difference do you think those reminders make to the French mindset, culture, and world view?
9. What is the most surprising thing you learned about France and French people?
10. The author makes many references to time in the book. What are some of the differences in how Americans and French use, view, and value time?
11. On several occasions the author writes about family's doing things together, teenagers willingly participating in family outings, and multi-generational activities as regular events. The author believes this is much more prevalent in France than in the U.S. Do you agree? If so, why do you think that's the case?
12. Why do you think the author and Kathryn broke up? Who do you think was mostly at fault? Why?
13. The author tells us his politics are liberal, yet on p. 194, the author says living in France makes him conservative and distrustful of change. Are you surprised? Has something like this ever happened to you?

Mark Greenside is available to speak by phone to reading groups. Please contact Andy Dodds—Andrew.dodds@simonandschuster.com.

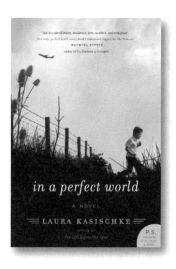

IN A PERFECT WORLD

AUTHOR: *Laura Kasischke*

PUBLISHER: Harper Perennial,
October 2009

WEBSITE: www.harperperennial.com

AVAILABLE IN:
Trade Paperback, 336 pages, $13.99
ISBN: 978-0-061-76611-4

SUBJECT: Relationships/Family/
Personal Challenges (Fiction)

PRAISE FOR LAURA KASISCHKE

"Kasischke's verses walk that perfect Plathian line between the every-day—making macaroni and cheese, getting pulled over for speeding—and the eternal, the plainspoken and the lyrical, the comfortable and the abyss of loss that lies just beneath it."—Time **magazine**

SUMMARY: *The Pilot's Wife* meets *The Road* in critically-acclaimed poet Laura Kasischke's new novel of marriage, motherhood, and the choices we make when we have no choices left. It was like a fairy tale. Jiselle almost couldn't believe it when *Captain* Mark Dorn, respected, handsome, tragic father, chose her to be his wife. The other flight attendants were jealous that she could quit her job, (since the outbreak of the Phoenix Flu filled a flight attendant's time with a million irritations), jealous that she would move into Mark Dorn's perfect cabin in the woods and become stepmother to Mark Dorn's three beautiful children. But it is no fairy tale. Jiselle begins to realize that Mark is away most the time, flying. And she's pretty sure that his daughters hate her. And the Phoenix Flu has begun to spread and will threaten Jiselle's marriage, her stepchildren, and the very lives they'd all imagined.

ABOUT THE AUTHOR: **Laura Kasischke** is the author of *Boy Heaven*, her first novel for teens, as well as *The Life Before Her Eyes, Be Mine*, and seven collections of poetry. She is an assistant professor at the University of Michigan, where she teaches creative writing. She lives in Chelsea, Michigan, with her husband and son.

1. Numerous fairy tales are interwoven with the plot of *In a Perfect World*. What are some of these tales, and how do they function within the story? How might this novel be read, itself, as a kind of fairy tale?

2. The unfolding of the love story between Jiselle and Mark is cut short with his quarantine and is soon overshadowed by her life with his children. How does this become its own romance, and in what ways does this shift comment on expectations regarding love and marriage?

3. How do you feel about the changes in Jiselle's character as the novel unfolds? How do you feel about the way she handles and reacts to the events of the novel, particularly the demands of step-motherhood?

4. Joy is a character who is never encountered in the novel, but who seems important nonetheless. How do you interpret her shadow-character, and how does Jiselle's "relationship" to her change during the course of the novel?

5. The author researched the Black Death in writing this book. Which events seem historically familiar? Which details seem to parallel contemporary concerns and events? Does the plot seem more fabulist than realistic? Can you imagine the kind of future the author has imagined?

6. Did you see Mark as a sympathetic character? Was Jiselle foolish to marry him?

7. At which moments in the novel do we see Jiselle's relationship to the children changing? Do you feel that, at some points, they become 'her' children? If so, where in the novel does this seem to occur?

8. Jiselle and the children are very isolated in this novel. Does this seem realistic to you? How do you feel about the few additional characters who figure in it: Jiselle's mother, Paul Temple, Tara Temple, the Schmidts?

9. What does the title, *In a Perfect World*, say to you about the themes and structure of the novel?

10. Is this an apocalyptic novel? What is your interpretation of the ending?

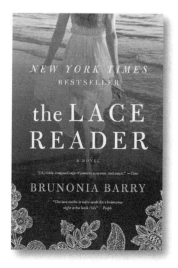

THE LACE READER

AUTHOR: **Brunonia Barry**

PUBLISHER: Harper paperbacks, 2009

WEBSITE: www.harpercollins.com
www.lacereader.com

AVAILABLE IN:
Trade Paperback, 400 pages, $14.99
ISBN: 978-0-06-162477-3

SUBJECT: Identity/Family/Relationships (Fiction)

"Drawing comparisons to memorable gothic novels, including Rebecca and The Thirteenth Tale. *Barry's modern-day story of Towner Whitney, who has the psychic gift to read the future in lace patterns, is equally complex but darker in subject matter. . . . Repressed memories emerge. Violent confrontations, reminiscent of the hysteria of the witch trials, explode in this complex novel . . . The novel's gripping and shocking conclusion is a testament to Barry's creativity."—USA* **Today**

"A spine-tingler set in Salem . . . [with] an irresistible pull. . . . The Lace Reader *is tailor-made for a boisterous night at the book club."—***People** *(***People** **Pick**)

*"[A] richly imagined saga of passion, suspense, and magic."—***Time** magazine

SUMMARY: Towner Whitney, the self-confessed unreliable narrator of *The Lace Reader*, hails from a family of Salem women who can read the future in the patterns in lace, and who have guarded a history of secrets going back generations, but the disappearance of two women brings Towner home to Salem and the truth about the death of her twin sister to light. *The Lace Reader* is a mesmerizing tale which spirals into a world of secrets, confused identities, lies and half-truths where the reader quickly finds it's nearly impossible to separate fact from fiction, but as Towner Whitney points out early on in the novel, "There are no accidents".

ABOUT THE AUTHOR: **Brunonia Barry**, born and raised in Massachusetts, studied literature and creative writing at Green Mountain College in Vermont and at the University of New Hampshire. Barry lives in Salem, Massachusetts, with her husband and their beloved Golden Retriever named Byzantium. Barry is at work on her second novel.

1. The author states that *The Lace Reader* is, at its core, about perception vs. reality. How does Rafferty's perception of Towner color his judgment of what she says and does? What about Rafferty's perception of Cal and his actions?

2. At the very start of *The Lace Reader,* Towner Whitney, the protagonist, tells the reader that she's a liar and that she's crazy. By the end of the book do you agree with her?

3. Eva reveals that she speaks in cliche so that her words do not influence the choices made by the recipients of her lace reading sessions. Do you think that's possible? Can a cliche be so over used that it loses its original meaning?

4. When May comments on the relationship between Rafferty and Towner, she states that they are too alike and predicts that "You won't just break apart. You'll send each other flying." Did you agree with that when you read it? And if so, in what ways are Towner and Rafferty alike?

5. Do you think that May's revival of the craft of handmade lace with the abused women on Yellow Dog Island is purely symbolic or could it be, in some way, very practical?

6. What role does religion play in the novel? Is there a difference between spirituality and religion? Between faith and blind faith?

7. Towner has a special bond with the dogs of Yellow Dog Island. Do you agree that people and animals can relate to each other in extraordinary ways?

8. How much does family history influence who a person becomes? Do you believe that certain traits or talents are genetic and can be inherited?

9. Is it possible that twins share a unique bond and how does being a twin affect Towner?

10. Can geography influence personality? For instance May lives on an island, does this say something about her?

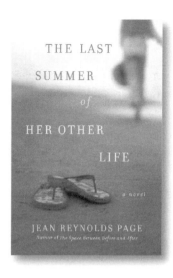

THE LAST SUMMER OF HER OTHER LIFE

AUTHOR: *Jean Reynolds Page*

PUBLISHER: Avon A, 2009

WEBSITE: www.avonbooks.com
www.jeanreynoldspage.com

AVAILABLE IN:
Trade Paperback, 320 pages, $13.99
ISBN: 978-0-061-45249-9

SUBJECT: Relationships/Women's Lives/
Personal Discovery (Fiction)

"Pleasant. . . . Page's knack for characterization . . . helps nudge things toward an appropriately affirmative ending."—**Publishers Weekly**

SUMMARY: From Jean Reynolds Page—the critically acclaimed author of *The Space Between Before and After* and one of the most compelling voices in contemporary women's fiction—comes a dazzling novel of loss and redemption, of relationships that damage and those that heal. Thirty-nine and pregnant by a man she's decided to leave behind in California, Jules' life is changing. Always the protected daughter, she must now relinquish that role and prepare to be a mother herself. But her efforts are upstaged by shocking allegations from a local teen in her North Carolina hometown. The boy has accused her of what the police are calling "inappropriate sexual contact." Three men rally in her defense: Lincoln, her brother, who flies in from New York to help her; Sam, her high school boyfriend, who after so many years still offers unconditional support; and Walt, the uncle of the teen, who charms Jules with his intelligence and unanticipated kindness. Her search for the truth about the troubled teenager becomes, for Jules, a first step toward discovering the woman she wishes to be.

ABOUT THE AUTHOR: **Jean Reynolds Page** is the author of *The Space Between Before and After*, *A Blessed Event* and *Accidental Happiness*. She grew up in North Carolina and graduated with a degree in journalism from The University of North Carolina at Chapel Hill. She worked as an arts publicist in New York City and for over a decade reviewed dance performances for numerous publications. She lives with her husband and three children to the Seattle area.

1. When Jules finds out she is pregnant with Thomas' child, she decides that, because he has repeatedly chosen to go off his medication for bipolar disorder (and as a result of this has exhibited dangerous behavior), she will not tell him about the baby. How do you feel about this decision? Do you think she made the right choice in order to protect her child or should he be told that he is a father in spite of the potential risks?

2. Lincoln and Jules had different experiences with their father, Jack Fuller. How did Jack's abuse affect who the two siblings became in their adult lives? How is Vick's experience similar to Lincoln's? How is it different? Why was the boy vulnerable to the particular type of abuse that he endured?

3. Walt tells Jules that she reminds him of a rodeo clown, something seemingly frivolous and fun, but with a fiercely serious purpose behind the charade. Jules believed that by maintaining the outward trappings of someone wild and unpredictable, she was shielding Lincoln by offering herself as a distraction. She wanted to protect her brother, first, from the anger of their father, and later, from the disapproval of the community. Do you think there were any additional, perhaps more self-serving, purposes for Jules' disguise? If so, what were they?

4. Jules is initially very upset with Sam for keeping the truth from her about the day their fathers died. Do you think she was justified in being angry with Sam, but not with Lincoln? Is it always better to know the truth about painful situations, or are there sometimes good reasons to stay quiet in order to protect someone?

5. What should happen to Tuni? Is she a victim of some sort of mental illness? Should this be taken into consideration, or are her actions beyond any such qualification?

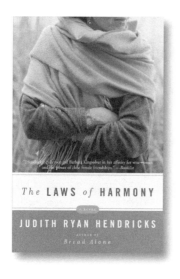

THE LAWS OF HARMONY

AUTHOR: *Judith Ryan Hendricks*

PUBLISHER: Harper paperbacks, 2009

WEBSITE: www.harpercollins.com
www.judihendricks.com

AVAILABLE IN:
Trade Paperback, 496 pages, $14.99
ISBN: 978-0-06-168736-5

SUBJECT: Family/Relationships/Identity (Fiction)

"Hendricks has an engaging narrative voice that will pull readers right into this story of a damaged woman who is more resilient than she realizes."
—Booklist

SUMMARY: In 1989, Sunny Cooper escaped to Albuquerque. Fourteen years later she's still there, struggling to make a living, to shore up her floundering relationship, and to forget her childhood on the New Mexico commune, Armonía, where a freak accident killed her younger sister, Mari.

Just when the "normal" life Sunny craves appears to be within reach, another accident—the sudden death of her fiancé, Michael, and revelations that their relationship was not what it seemed—will turn her world upside down. Once again, Sunny escapes, this time to the Pacific Northwest town of Harmony on San Miguel Island. When a surprising discovery sparks an emotional encounter for Sunny with her estranged mother, Gwen, she must re-examine the truth of her memories. Only by making peace with the past can Sunny finally step out of its shadow and into a new life.

ABOUT THE AUTHOR: **Judith Ryan Hendricks**, a former journalist, copywriter, computer instructor, travel agent, waitress, and baker, is the author of three previous novels, including the bestseller *Bread Alone.* She and her husband live in New Mexico.

1. What does Sunny Cooper's flexible assortment of occupations— voice-over artist, personal errand runner, obsessive baker—suggest about her personality and her professional focus?

2. How do the suspicious circumstances surrounding Michael Graham's death and his behavior prior to his disappearance make him seem like a stranger to Sunny?

3. How do the detailed descriptions of food and cooking in *The Laws of Harmony* affect your reading experience? Which were most memorable to you and why?

4. Why does Betsy Chambliss conceal her betrayal from Sunny, and could there be any possible justification for her behavior?

5. How does the tragic death of her younger sister, Mari, factor into Sunny's feelings about growing up in the commune in Armonía?

6. Sunny can't wait to get away from Armonía, but after almost fourteen years on her own, the normality and stability she craves still elude her. Why is this? To what extent is the summer idyll with her grandparents in California responsible for her sense of living an unmoored life?

7. Why do you think the author chose to explore the strange coincidence of Sunny's having been raised in Armonía, and her having turned up in a town called Harmony? What does this convergence suggest, and to what extent do you think the names might be intended ironically?

8. How would you characterize Sunny's feelings about her mother, Gwen, returning to her life? To what extent is their relationship irretrievably fractured?

9. What does JT's reaction to the news of Sunny's pregnancy reveal about his character and their romantic potential as a couple?

10. What do you think the ending of the book suggests for Sunny, her future life in San Miguel, and her relationships with JT, Gwen, and the others on whom she has come to depend?

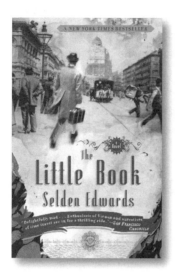

THE LITTLE BOOK

AUTHOR: *Selden Edwards*

PUBLISHER: Plume Books, 2009

WEBSITE: www.penguingroup.com

AVAILABLE IN:
Trade Paperback, 416 pages, $15.00
ISBN: 978-0-452-29551-3

SUBJECT: Adventure/Fantasy/Mystery (Fiction)

"This novel ends up a sweet, wistful elegy to the fantastic promise and failed hopes of the 20th century."—**Publishers Weekly**

SUMMARY: *The Little Book* is the extraordinary tale of Wheeler Burden, California-exiled heir of the famous Boston banking Burdens, philosopher, student of history, legend's son, rock idol, writer, lover of women, recluse, half-Jew, and Harvard baseball hero. In 1988 he is forty-seven, living in San Francisco. Suddenly he is—still his modern self—wandering in a city and time he knows mysteriously well: fin de siècle Vienna. It is 1897, precisely ninety-one years before his last memory and a half-century before his birth.

The truth at the center of Wheeler's dislocation in time remains a stubborn mystery that will take months of exploration and a lifetime of memories to unravel and that will, in the end, reveal nothing short of the eccentric Burden family's unrivaled impact on the very course of the coming century. *The Little Book* is a masterpiece of unequaled storytelling that announces Selden Edwards as one of the most dazzling, original, entertaining, and inventive novelists of our time.

ABOUT THE AUTHOR: **Selden Edwards** began writing *The Little Book* as a young English teacher in 1974, and continued to layer and refine the manuscript until its completion in 2007. It is his first novel. He lives in Santa Barbara, California.

1. Why did the author choose Flora to fill the role of narrator? How might the book be different if Wheeler told the story in the first person?

2. Before reading *The Little Book*, what did you know about the fin de siècle period of European history? What are some of the things you've learned? Why do you think the author chose to portray this era in the novel?

3. Discuss the first and surnames of the book's major characters. Is it significant that Wheeler adopted his first name from his childhood nickname in baseball? Or that he assumed the name "Harry Truman" in Vienna? What literal "burdens" are carried by each of the Burden men?

4. Discuss the female characters in *The Little Book*. What impact did the women in his life have on Wheeler? Compare and contrast figures such as Wheeler's mother, Flora, and his grandmother, Weezie (Eleanor).

5. Throughout the book, the narrator notes seemingly innocuous conversations or events that later prove to be momentous. What did you think of this plot device? Did it enhance your reading experience, or would you have preferred these plot points to reveal themselves more organically?

6. Consider the role of books in *The Little Book*. Why is the recording of history—such as the writing of Esterhazy's "Random Notes," Wheeler's journal, Weezie's letter to Flora, or other examples—such an important task?

7. While in Vienna and in need of money, Wheeler could have chosen a variety of ways to make a fortune given his intimate knowledge of the future. But he chooses to create a Frisbee—why? How did it prove to be a noteworthy invention?

8. Talk about the great love affairs of the novel, like those of Dilly and Flora, modern Wheeler and Joan, and Vienna Wheeler and Weezie. What are parallels between some of these pairings?

9. What did you think of the book's ending, when the identity of Wheeler's San Francisco assailant was revealed? Did you suspect who it really was?

10. Talk about the idea of "hero" and "legend," two words that are often used to describe Dilly but that also apply to Wheeler. What does it mean to be a hero or a legend? How are Dilly and Wheeler similar in this regard?

11. What brought Wheeler to 1897 Vienna? If you had the opportunity to go back in time, what period of history would you choose to live in? Would you intend to alter history's course? Why or why not?

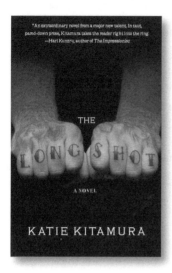

THE LONGSHOT

AUTHOR: *Katie Kitamura*

PUBLISHER: Free Press, 2009

WEBSITE: www.simonandschuster.com
www.katiekitamura.com

AVAILABLE IN:
Trade Paperback, 208 pages, $14.00
ISBN: 978-1-439-10752-2

SUBJECT: Identity/Relationships/Personal
Discovery (Fiction)

"The Longshot *takes the reader into the minds, hearts, and bodies of two highly dedicated and taciturn men. . . . Her writing is spellbinding . . . in its power. Kitamura is a genuine discovery."*—**Booklist** (starred review)

"*Spare and beautifully written. . . . [Kitamura] brings a physicality to her story with descriptions of the action so vivid the reader feels the pain of every punch and kick."*—***Publishers Weekly***

SUMMARY: Cal and his trainer, Riley, are on their way to Mexico for a make-or-break rematch with legendary fighter Rivera. Four years ago, Cal became the only mixed martial arts fighter to take Rivera the distance—but the fight nearly ended him. Only Riley, who has been at his side for the last ten years, knows how much that fight changed things for Cal. And only Riley really knows what's now at stake, for both of them.

Katie Kitamura's brilliant and stirring debut novel follows Cal and Riley through the three fraught days leading up to this momentous match, as each privately begins to doubt that Cal can win. The looming fight becomes every challenge each of us has ever taken on, no matter how uncertain the outcome.

In hypnotic, pared-down prose, *The Longshot* offers a striking portrait of two men striving to stay true to themselves and each other in the only way they know how.

ABOUT THE AUTHOR: **Katie Kitamura** was born in 1979, and divides her time between New York and London. *The Longshot* is her first novel.

1. A number of times over the course of the story, a certain question comes up: What went wrong in that fateful fight between Cal and Rivera four years ago? Discuss Cal and Riley's conflicting opinions on what actually happened. Who do you think is right?

2. Riley comments that in the beginning of Cal's career, Cal got so used to winning that he just thought it was "the way it was"(p. 16). How did that make losing to Rivera that much harder for him? Why has it taken him so long to get back into serious fighting?

3. What was the result of Murray and Rivera's fight? Do you think Cal would rather follow in Murray's footsteps than risk another defeat by Rivera? Why do you think he chooses to fight him again?

4. Cal and Riley each experience a fight-or-flight impulse during the twenty-four hours leading up to the fight. Why does each of them decide to stay? How do you think the novel would have turned out if one of them had fled? What would it have meant to the one who got left behind?

5. Why does Riley put so much pressure on himself to turn Cal into a champion? Do you think this blindly leads him into believing that Cal can win the rematch?

6. Even though he has never been knocked out, why do you think Cal "guessed he knew the feeling" (p. 23)? Why is it so important to Cal to remain standing in the final fight?

7. Having read Kitamura's work, do you agree with her statement that "there was nothing simple about a fight" (p. 27)? Did *The Longshot* change your perspective on the world of mixed martial arts fighting, on the people involved in it, and on the fighting itself? Why or why not?

8. Do you agree with Kitamura's assertion that "a fight was just a series of logical conclusions" (p.111)? If so, how do you feel about Cal's claim that habit overrides fear, logic and need (p. 139)?

9. Do you think Cal dies at the end of the book? Why or why not?

Katie Kitamura is available to speak by phone to reading groups. Please contact Jill Siegel—Jill.Siegel@simonandschuster.com

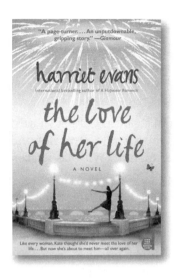

THE LOVE OF HER LIFE

AUTHOR: *Harriet Evans*

PUBLISHER: Downtown Press, 2009

WEBSITE:www.simonandschuster.com

AVAILABLE IN:
Trade Paperback, 448 pages, $15.00
ISBN: 978-1-4391-1315-8

SUBJECT: Love & Romance/Family/
Relationships (Fiction)

*"Harriet Evans' latest page turner. . . . An unputdownable, gripping story of life, loss, and one girl's search for happiness."—**Glamour***

*"You will cry. Guaranteed."—**Company** magazine*

SUMMARY: In London, Kate Miller had an enviable life: an exciting job at a fashion magazine, an engagement and a wedding to plan. Then it all fell apart—spectacularly, painfully, and forever. That was three years ago . . . and she fled to New York City to live with her mother and stepfather.

Now Kate is a true New Yorker, in love with the pace and rhythm of Manhattan. But deep down, she knows her life is in a holding pattern, that there is something—someone—more to love. But when her father becomes ill, Kate realizes it's time to return and face the friends and the memories she left behind. What really happened before Kate left London? Can she pick up the pieces and allow herself to love life again?

ABOUT THE AUTHOR: **Harriet Evans** is the author of the international bestseller *Going Home*, available from Downtown Press. She lives in London, where she works in publishing and is writing her next novel.

1. When preparing to return to London, Kate remarks, "It will be hard. . . . I had to go back sometime . . . Just wish it wasn't for this, that's all" (p. 12). If not for her father's illness, do you think Kate would have gone back? Would she ever have returned to her old self in New York, or did she need to go back to London to rediscover herself? Do you agree with her that she is "too good at running away" (p. 21)?

2. Discuss Kate's "new self " vs. her "old self " (p. 14). Which Kate do you like better? Which one do you think Kate likes better? Would "old" Kate have shrugged off Andrew the way "new" Kate had at the beginning of the novel?

3. How does the author's use of foreshadowing intensify the moment when the reader finds out what really happened in Kate's past? How do the flashbacks add to this element? How would the book have been different if it started right after Kate graduated from college?

4. Kate and Mac's first encounter results in nothing more than a one-night stand, or so it seems. Why do you think Kate remarked that that night she had a "strange sense of certainty, one that she never got back again" (p. 108)? Does she ever get that certainty back?

5. Sue Jordan, Kate's old boss, criticizes Kate for her current career choice. What is Kate's response? Why do you think she initially resisted Sue's offer to write the column? What does Sue mean when she says, "we're all the same, you know, it's just different versions of being the same" (p. 180)? Do you agree?

6. As the events of the novel unfold, it appears that Kate is becoming deeply entrenched in the city she tried to forget. How do her struggles with staying or leaving affect her interactions with Mac, Zoe, Francesca, and her family? Do you agree that "if the last few weeks had taught her anything, it was that she . . . had to start being brave and get out there" (p. 354)?

7. Kate goes through a tremendous transformation throughout the novel. What makes Kate become comfortable with the person she is? Or does she never reach that milestone?

8. Which experience do you think helped shape Kate the most? When is she at her weakest? Her strongest?

9. Did the ending of *The Love of Her Life* surprise you? Is this where Kate is meant to be? Is this the man whom she is meant to be with? Do you think she might run again, or is she here to stay? And why?

MADNESS
A Bipolar Life

AUTHOR: *Marya Hornbacher*

PUBLISHER: Mariner Books, 2009

WEBSITE: www.hmhbooks.com
www.maryahornbacher.com

AVAILABLE IN:
Trade Paperback, 320 pages, $14.95
ISBN: 978-0-547-23780-0

SUBJECT: Biography/Women's Lives/
Personal Challenges (Memoir)

SUMMARY: When Marya Hornbacher published her first book, *Wasted: A Memoir of Anorexia and Bulimia*, she did not yet have the piece of shattering knowledge that would finally make sense of the chaos of her life. At age twenty-four, Hornbacher was diagnosed with Type I rapid-cycle bipolar, the most severe form of bipolar disorder.

In *Madness*, in her trademark wry and utterly self-revealing voice, Hornbacher tells her new story. Through scenes of astonishing visceral and emotional power, she takes us inside her own desperate attempts to counteract violently careening mood swings by self-starvation, substance abuse, numbing sex, and self-mutilation. How Hornbacher fights her way up from a madness that all but destroys her, and what it is like to live in a difficult and sometimes beautiful life and marriage—where bipolar always beckons—is at the center of this brave and heart-stopping memoir. And Hornbacher's fiercely self-aware portrait of her own bipolar as early as age four will powerfully change, too, the current debate on whether bipolar in children actually exists.

ABOUT THE AUTHOR: **Marya Hornbacher** is the author of the Pulitzer Prize-nominated national bestseller *Wasted: A Memoir of Anorexia and Bulimia*, a book that remains an intensely read classic, and the acclaimed novel *The Center of Winter*. An award-winning journalist, she lectures nationally on writing and mental health and lives in Minneapolis, Minnesota.

1. How much does Hornbacher's self-image, or her very identity for that matter, revolve around her "madness"? Does Hornbacher eventually succeed in forging an identity separate from the effects the disorder? Can you describe Hornbacher's personality, her tone as a narrator, and even her actions in a way that is devoid of the traits and the descriptive terms of bipolar? Can the two be separated?

2. Do you think Hornbacher's family history ultimately helped her find a kind of acceptance and support early in life that she wouldn't have had in other circumstances? Do you think her parents have any responsibility for the course Hornbacher's early life took?

3. Do you view actions that in other circumstances might end up labeled as extreme teenage rebellion differently than you would if someone without a mental health diagnosis was leading the life Hornbacher described? Are you more sympathetic or more skeptical? Do you think a lot of people would see Hornbacher in this period of her life as her first psychiatrist did, just as "a very angry little girl"?

4. Hornbacher describes several instances in which she resorted to manipulation and deceit. Time after time, Hornbacher gets people to think she is well enough to be on her own, making her own decisions. Do you see this in some sense as a failure of the system, or is it more of a marker of Hornbacher's intelligence and ability? In what other instances does she take control in ways that turn out to be harmful? What are other reoccurring patterns and cycles of behavior in *Madness*?

5. What would you consider overtly crazy behavior? Sane behavior? How much are your perceptions based on your own experiences of societal norms? How much of what you consider "crazy" comes from what you are familiar with in movies, books, and popular culture?

6. How does receiving a diagnosis of mental illness feel different from being diagnosed with other illnesses? Do you think the power of the diagnosis contributes to Hornbacher's initial, destructive denial?

7. As Hornbacher accepts her own diagnosis, do you think she is also trying to change public preconceptions about mental disorders? And if so, does she succeed?

8. What do you think are the challenges mental illness poses to a relationship, particularly a marriage? Why and how do you think Jeff and Marya's relationship has lasted?

9. The disease is part of who Hornbacher is and has a large role in shaping the person she has become. Do you think that other people with mental illness would agree? How do you think doctors and mental health professionals would react to Hornbacher's statement?

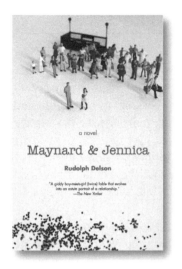

MAYNARD AND JENNICA

AUTHOR: **Rudolph Delson**

PUBLISHER: Mariner Books, 2009

WEBSITE: www.hmhbooks.com
         www.rudolphdelson.com

AVAILABLE IN:
Trade Paperback, 304 pages, $13.95
ISBN: 978-0-547-08571-5

SUBJECT: Humor/Love & Romance/Family
(Fiction)

"Delson's prose shimmers when describing the magic and romance of falling in love in New York."—Publishers Weekly

"Delson's clever debut is sharp and energetic, a highly original contemporary love story set against New York's invigorating urban landscape."
—Booklist

"Boldly inventive . . . this work has something fresh that needs to be embraced and will resonate with a wide audience."—Library Journal

SUMMARY: A wildly original debut, *Maynard and Jennica* is both a hilarious urban comedy and a captivating love story. In the summer of 2000, while riding the uptown number 6 train, the musician/filmmaker Maynard Gogarty first encounters the beautiful Jennica Green. Though their initial meeting is brief, when fate next brings them together a romance ensues, and as with most things in life, everyone has an opinion.

Delson tells the story of this improbable love affair through the voices of Maynard and Jennica, along with their family, friends, and assorted characters (among them two attorneys, three journalists, and a rap star) pulled into their dizzying orbit. He brings to life a pair of lovers who are flawed, complex, at once eccentric and deeply familiar—and in whose story we continue to feel invested long after we've turned the last page.

ABOUT THE AUTHOR: **Rudolph Delson** was raised in San Jose, graduated from Stanford, and currently lives in Brooklyn.

1. Do you consider this novel a comedy? Comedy is a term more often associated with the theatrical arts. In what ways is *Maynard & Jennica* more like a play than a novel?
2. What do some of the other characters think of Maynard? How do you account for these opposing views? What is your impression of Maynard?
3. Everyone in this novel, even minor characters, birds, and the long deceased, has an opinion and gets their say. What affect does this have on your reading? How does it help, or hinder your understanding of the two main characters?
4. Maynard lives his life according to his idea of dignity. What does it mean to be dignified? In what ways does Maynard succeed or fail?
5. Jennica, meanwhile, wants to live an illustrious life. What do you think Jennica really wants? How does Jennica's search for the illustrious and Maynard's strivings to be dignified complement each other?
6. Why does Jennica find Maynard so attractive the second time they meet? Who is Jennica running away from when she meets Maynard? Why doesn't she run away from Maynard—or does she?
7. Maynard is arrested for poisoning trees in the park across the street from his apartment building. Why isn't he more concerned about the possibility of going to jail? Why does he do it in the first place and how does he get out of it?
8. "Patriotism is always in such—bad taste." And so begins Maynard's "unacceptable" response to the events of September 11th. How did Maynard's words make you feel? Could you find any truth in what he said? Why do you think Maynard reacted this way?
9. A number of different arguments take place at the Gogarty cabin on the 17th of September, 2001. What are they each about? What is the argument between Maynard and Jennica about on the surface, and what do you think they're really fighting about?
10. Maynard's mother calls her son "Manny," Jennica calls him "Arnie," Ana calls him "Gogi." Why do they all have different names for him? Why does no one call him Maynard?
11. What romantic beliefs does Jennica hold? How does Maynard, as Jennica says, solve the "Jennica Green marriage problem"?
12. Who is Ana Kaganova and where does she really come from? What lies does she tell? Do you consider her a villain?
13. Why does Jennica cheat on Maynard with George Hanamoto? Were you surprised? How do Maynard and Jennica win each other back?
14. What changes that allows Jennica to move back to California at the end of the book? What is her idea of success?

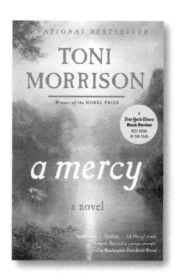

A MERCY

AUTHOR: *Toni Morrison*

PUBLISHER: Vintage Books, 2009

WEBSITE: www.ReadingGroupCenter.com

AVAILABLE IN:
Trade Paperback, 224 pages, $15.00
ISBN: 978-0-307-27676-6

SUBJECT: American History/Relationships/
Personal Challenges (Fiction)

"*Spellbinding. . . . Dazzling. . . .* [A Mercy] *stands alongside Beloved as a unique triumph.*"—*The Washington Post Book World*

SUMMARY: In the 1680s the slave trade in the Americas is still in its infancy. Jacob Vaark is an Anglo-Dutch trader and adventurer, with a small holding in the harsh North. Despite his distaste for dealing in "flesh," he takes a small slave girl in part payment for a bad debt from a plantation owner in Catholic Maryland. This is Florens, who can read and write and might be useful on his farm. Rejected by her mother, Florens looks for love, first from Lina, an older servant woman at her new master's house, and later from the handsome blacksmith, an African, never enslaved, who comes riding into their lives.

A Mercy reveals what lies beneath the surface of slavery. But at its heart, like *Beloved*, it is the ambivalent, disturbing story of a mother and a daughter—a mother who casts off her daughter in order to save her, and a daughter who may never exorcise that abandonment.

ABOUT THE AUTHOR: **Toni Morrison** is the Robert F. Goheen Professor of Humanities, Emerita, at Princeton University. She has received the National Book Critics Circle Award and the Pulitzer Prize. In 1993 she was awarded the Nobel Prize in Literature. She lives in Rockland County, New York, and Princeton, New Jersey.

1. In what sense is Florens' story a confession? What are the dreamlike "curiosities" it is filled with?
2. What does *A Mercy* reveal about Colonial America that is startling and new? In what ways does Morrison give this period in our history an emotional depth that cannot be found in text books?
3. What do the characters reveal about themselves through the way they speak? What are the advantages of such a multivocal narrative over one told through a single voice?
4. How does Jacob's attitude toward his slaves/workers differ from that of the farmer who owns Florens's mother?
5. What does the novel as a whole reveal about the precarious position of women, European and African, free and enslaved, in late-7th-century America?
6. In what ways is "civilized" England more savage than "savage" America?
7. What role does the love story between Florens and the blacksmith play in the novel? Why does the blacksmith tell Florens that she is "a slave by choice" (page 141)?
8. How are Christians depicted in the novel? How do they regard Florens, and black people generally?
9. Why does Florens's mother urge Jacob to take her? Why does she consider his doing so a mercy? What does her decision say about the conditions in which she and so many others like her were forced to live?
10. In what ways is *A Mercy* about the condition of being orphaned? What is the literal and symbolic significance of being orphaned or abandoned in the novel?
11. Why does Morrison choose to end the novel in the voice of Florens' mother? How does the ending alter or intensify all that has come before it?
12. Why is it important to have a visceral, emotional grasp of what life was like, especially for Africans, Native Americans, and women, in Colonial America? In what ways has American culture tried to forget or whitewash this history?
13. Did you see the stunning twist at the novel's conclusion coming? If so, when and why? If not, why do you think it blindsided you?
14. How do the stories of the women in *A Mercy* serve as a prequel to the stories of the women in *Beloved*, which is set two centuries later?

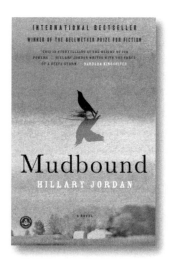

MUDBOUND

AUTHOR: *Hillary Jordan*

PUBLISHER: Algonquin Books, 2009

WEBSITE: www.algonquin.com
www.hillaryjordan.com

AVAILABLE IN:
Trade Paperback, 340 pages, $13.95
ISBN: 978-1-56512-677-0

SUBJECT: Family/Social Issues/History
(Fiction)

"A compelling family tragedy, a confluence of romantic attraction and racial hatred that eventually falls like an avalanche. . . . The last third of the book is downright breathless."—The Washington Post Book World

SUMMARY: In Jordan's prize-winning debut, prejudice takes many forms, both subtle and brutal. It is 1946, and city-bred Laura McAllan is trying to raise her children on her husband's Mississippi Delta farm—a place she finds foreign and frightening. In the midst of the family's struggles, two young men return from the war to work the land. Jamie McAllan, Laura's brother-in-law, is everything her husband is not—charming, handsome, and haunted by his memories of combat and Ronsel Jackson, eldest son of the black sharecroppers who live on the McAllan farm. It is the unlikely friendship of these brothers-in-arms that drives this powerful novel.

The men and women of each family relate their versions of events, and we are drawn into their lives as they become players in a tragedy on the grandest scale. As Kingsolver says of Hillary Jordan, "Her characters walked straight out of 1940s Mississippi and into the part of my brain where sympathy and anger and love reside, leaving my heart racing. They are with me still."

ABOUT THE AUTHOR: **Hillary Jordan's** first novel, *Mudbound*, won the 2006 Bellwether Prize for Fiction and was the New Atlantic Independent Booksellers Association Fiction Book of the Year for 2008. She lives in Tivoli, New York.

1. Discuss the ways in which the Mississippi Delta functions as a character in the novel and how each of the other characters relates to it.
2. *Mudbound* is a chorus, told in six different voices. How do the changes in perspective affect your understanding of the story? Are all six voices equally sympathetic? Reliable? Pappy is the only main character who has no narrative voice. Why do you think the author chose not to let him speak?
3. Who gets to speak and who is silent or silenced is a central theme, the silencing of Ronsel being the most literal and brutal example. Discuss the ways in which this theme plays out for the other characters. What are the consequences of Jamie's inability to speak to his family about the horrors he experienced in the war? How does speaking or not speaking confer power or take it away?
4. The story is narrated by two farmers, two wives and mothers, and two soldiers. Compare and contrast the ways in which these parallel characters, black and white, view and experience the world.
5. What is the significance of the title? In what ways are each of the characters bound—by the land, by circumstance, by tradition, by the law, by their own limitations? How much of this binding is inescapable and how much is self-imposed?
6. Would Laura have thought of herself as racist, and if not, why not? How do the racial views of Laura, Jamie, Henry, and Pappy affect your sympathy for them?
7. The novel deals with many thorny issues: racism, sexual politics, infidelity, war. The characters weigh in on these issues, but what about the author? Does she have a discernable perspective, and if so, how does she convey it?
8. We know very early in the book that something terrible is going to befall Ronsel. How does this sense of inevitability affect the story? Where would you place the turning point for Ronsel? Who else is complicit in what happens to him, and why?
9. In reflecting on some of the more difficult moral choices made by the characters—what would you have done in those same situations? Are there some moral positions that are absolute, or should we take into account things like time and place when making judgments?
10. Why do you think the author chose to have Ronsel address you, the reader, directly, in the last chapter? Do you believe he overcomes the formidable obstacles facing him and finds "something like happiness"? If so, why doesn't the author just say so explicitly? Would a less ambiguous ending have been more or less satisfying?

NOW & THEN

AUTHOR: *Jacqueline Sheehan*

PUBLISHER: Avon A, 2009

WEBSITE: www.avonbooks.com
www.jacquelinesheehan.com

AVAILABLE IN:
Trade Paperback, 386 pages, $13.99
ISBN: 978-0-061-54778-2

SUBJECT: Relationships/Animals/History
(Fiction)

"Sheehan . . . reminds us that those who came before were no less savvy in their time than we like to think of ourselves today and that by accepting the past, we might just change the future. For readers looking for a well-written story with just a touch of blarney."—**Library Journal**

SUMMARY: Living a dog's life . . . now and then. Anna O'Shea has failed at marriage, shed her job at a law firm, and she's trying to re-create herself when she and her recalcitrant nephew are summoned to the past in a manner that nearly destroys them. Her twenty-first-century skills pale as she struggles to find her nephew in nineteenth-century Ireland. For one of them, the past is brutally difficult, filled with hunger and struggle. For the other, the past is filled with privilege, status, and a reprieve from the crushing pain of present-day life. For both Anna and her nephew, the past offers them a chance at love. Will every choice they make reverberate down through time? And do Irish Wolfhounds carry the soul of the ancient celts? Mystical, charming, and fantastic, *The New York Times* bestselling author Jacqueline Sheehan's *Now & Then* is a poignant and beautiful tale of a remarkable journey. It is a miraculous evocation of a breathtaking place in a volatile age filled with rich, unforgettable, deeply human characters and one unforgettable dog named Madigan.

ABOUT THE AUTHOR: **Jacqueline Sheehan, Ph.D.**, is a fiction writer and essayist. She is *The New York Times* bestselling author of *Lost & Found* and *Truth*, based on the life of Sojourner Truth. She teaches writing at Grub Street in Boston, Writers in Progress in Florence, Massachusetts, and she offers international writing retreats in Jamaica.

1. Both main characters, Anna and Joseph, are troubled in their present lives. How does their leap into the past offer them a second chance?

2. Irish wolfhounds, which were close to extinction by the middle of the 19th Century, were said to carry the spirits of the ancient Celts. Discuss why the dogs appear to refuse to breed on the Colonel's estate.

3. The outer trapping of Joseph's life improve dramatically with his new life. What are the factors that initially leave him blind to the nature of the colonel? What are the elements that make it hard for him to understand the big picture?

4. Privilege and class affect Anna and Joseph in profoundly different ways. They even change physically in ways that are influenced by their situations. How do Anna and Joseph represent the difference between the Irish and land-rich English?

5. The Irish are never quite who they seem to be in this story. What strategies do the Irish use to communicate and survive while living in an occupied nation?

6. Glenis is Anna's greatest friend and defender. What affect does Glenis' sacrifice have on Anna?

7. In what ways do Anna and Joseph have more advantages or disadvantages because they come from the future?

8. Biddy Early, Deirdre and Taleen all have "the sight" to greater or lesser degrees. Their influence is understated but essential. Which characters would not have survived without them?

9. Friendship and love figure prominently in this story. Although we only learn about the last days of Anna's marriage to Steve, how does it compare to her relationship with Donal? Why is she so tempted to stay in the past?

10. The story starts at the beginning—or does it? Biddy Early describes time as a spiral that is somewhat beyond our comprehension. How did you understand the nature of time travel in this story? Is it important to understand every detail of it? How did the spiraling of time, and a curse from the past, affect this Irish American family?

11. Speculate on Anna's life after she returns to present day Ireland. How has time travel changed her?

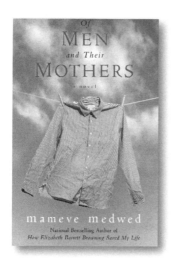

OF MEN AND THEIR MOTHERS

AUTHOR: *Mameve Medwed*

PUBLISHER: Avon A, 2009

WEBSITE: www.avonbooks.com
www.mamevemedwed.com

AVAILABLE IN:
Trade Paperback, 304 pages, $13.99
ISBN: 978-0-06-083122-6

SUBJECT: Family/Relationships/Personal
Discovery (Fiction)

*"[Medwed] is especially adroit at crafting dialogue that keeps the narrative humming. . . . This mother-in-law from Hades is an inspired comic creation. . . . Medwed refuses to let the stereotypes stand. Her characters don't remain inside convenient little boxes."—**The Boston Globe***

SUMMARY: All men have mothers . . .

It's a truth that the newly unhyphenated Maisie Grey has learned the hard way. After getting rid of her mama's-boy husband, she happily settles down with her teenage son, Tommy. But she's still stuck with the hovering presence of her impossible mother-in-law, Tommy's grandmother, who refuses to exit the family stage gracefully. Trying to keep it together with her own business and a new relationship with a man who still lives in—*where else but?*—his mother's house, Maisie struggles to learn from the MIL-from-hell. She vows that when Tommy brings someone home, she'll be loving, empathetic, and supportive. But then along comes completely unsuitable September Silva—with her too-short skirts, black nail polish, and stay-out-all-night attitude—who is forcing Maisie to take a flinty, clear-eyed new look at what it means to be a mother.

ABOUT THE AUTHOR: **Mameve Medwed** is also the author of *Mail, Host Family, The End of an Error*, and *How Elizabeth Barrett Browning Saved My Life* (which received a 2007 Massachusetts Book Honor Award). Her stories, essays, and reviews have appeared in many publications including the *Missouri Review, Redbook, The Boston Globe, Yankee, The Washington Post*, and *Newsday*. She and her husband have two sons and live in Cambridge, Massachusetts.

1. Are mother/son relationships more fraught than daughter/son ones?
2. Both Rex and Gabriel are mama's boys. What's the difference between them?
3. Is Maisie doomed to repeat history with Gabriel? Does the influence of a man's mother linger after she's dead? How do you predict things will work out for Maisie and Gabriel?
4. Should Maisie have taken in September—what would you have done? What is the best way to deal with a son's girlfriend you disapprove of?
5. Did Maisie handle the powder in the backpack in a reasonable way? Can you suggest alternatives?
6. Some of you may know that Seamus is a repeat character from Mameve Medwed's first novel. Does or does that not work for you? Does his presence add something?
7. How do the symbols of breast milk and chicken potpies take on meaning throughout the book?
8. How did Maisie's mentoring of Darlene change Darlene? And change Maisie, too?
9. What role does class play in this novel in relation to Maisie's background, the Pollocks, Darlene and Carlene, September, Gabriel. What are the telling symbols of class—interiors, clothes, residences, and how do they work out in the course of the book. How does snobbery affect the relationships among the characters?
10. Name the parallels between all the mothers and sons, daughters and mothers-in-law in the book.
11. Is Ina Pollock truly the mother-in-law from hell or is there some redemption?
12. Would you consider Factotum, Inc. a suitable career for Maisie? What does this choice of profession show about Maisie other than the potential for comedy?
13. Who gets their just desserts? Rex, Maisie? Ina? Seamus?
14. How does humor work to mitigate painful things? What are the serious themes and issues in the book underlying the comedy?

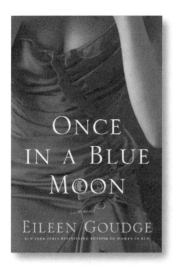

ONCE IN A BLUE MOON

AUTHOR: *Eileen Goudge*

PUBLISHER: Vanguard Press, October 2009
A member of The Perseus Books Group

WEBSITE: www.eileengoudge.com
www.vanguardpressbooks.com

AVAILABLE IN:
Hardcover, 320 pages, $24.95
ISBN: 978-1-593-15534-6

SUBJECT: Family/Relationships/Identity
(Fiction)

PRAISE FOR EILEEN GOUDGE

"Eileen Goudge writes like a house on fire, creating characters you come to love and hate to leave."—**Nora Roberts**

SUMMARY: From the *The New York Times* bestselling author of *Woman in Red and The Diary* comes another emotionally charged family drama, focusing on two sisters and their turbulent lives. While growing up, it was Lindsay's job to look after her little sister, Kerrie Ann. When the girls' stripper mom is sent to prison, their neighbor, a retired exotic dancer by the name of Miss Honi Love, fights to spare them from foster care, but to no avail.

Lindsay was adopted by a loving couple. Thirty years later, Lindsay is still trying to reconnect with her long-lost sister. Unbeknownst to her, Kerrie Ann has led a very different life, bounced from one foster home to the next. Now, newly sober, Kerrie Ann is fighting to regain custody of her little girl.

When the sisters are finally reunited, the two very different women clash. As Lindsay and Kerrie Ann engage in the fiercest battles of their lives—while each embarks on a journey of the heart with the unlikeliest of men—they are drawn together, restoring belief in the unshakable bond of family.

ABOUT THE AUTHOR: **Eileen Goudge** is *The New York Times* bestselling author whose novels include *The Diary, Domestic Affairs, Woman in Red, One Last Dance, Garden of Lies*, and *Thorns of Truth*. She lives with her husband, entertainment reporter Sandy Kenyon, in New York City.

1. "Once in a blue moon" conventionally refers to a situation that is rare or unique. Discuss a time in your life that was unusual and probably will never happen again. What makes *Once in a Blue Moon* unique?

2. *Once in a Blue Moon* examines the challenges and triumphs of sisterhood. What has your relationship been like with your siblings? How is the relationship with a sibling different than with a friend? What makes relationships with siblings easier and harder than with friends?

3. Kerrie Ann, newly sober, shows up at the Blue Moon Book Café unexpectedly, hoping that Lindsay will help her. How would you have responded to Kerrie Ann? The younger sister continues to make poor choices, frustrating an already stressed Lindsay. What would you have done in Lindsay's place? Describe a time in your life when you've had to help a family member.

4. What character in the book do you most identify with and why? What character frustrates you and why?

5. Everyone has had challenges, made mistakes and done things they've regretted. What do you think Kerrie Ann learned? What mistakes does Lindsay make? What does she learn? What have you learned from your own mistakes?

6. Lindsay loves Grant, but can't commit to marrying him. She quickly falls for Randall. How has love surprised you in your life? Describe a time in your life when you rejected love.

7. Miss Honi acts as a mother when Lindsay and Kerrie Ann need her, providing abundant love and support. Who have been significant women in your life? Who's been there for you when you needed unconditional love?

8. Like author Eileen Goudge, Ollie bakes to relax and express his love for others. What are some creative ways that you express yourself and your love for others?

9. Lindsay loves running the Blue Moon Bay Book Café with her family and friends, but struggles to make ends meet. Should she have sold the bookstore? Why or why not? As an independent bookstore, what does the shop offer Lindsay, her family, and the community? Do you shop at independently owned stores? Why or why not?

10. *Once in a Blue Moon* tackles several challenging issues–addiction, recovery, child neglect, foster care, adoption, loss, infidelity–with great compassion and understanding. What message did you find in this story?

ONE WEEK IN DECEMBER

AUTHOR: *Holly Chamberlin*

PUBLISHER: Kensington Books, 2009

WEBSITE: www.hollychamberlin.com
www.kensingtonbooks.com

AVAILABLE IN:
Trade Paperback, 352 pages, $14.00
ISBN: 978-0-7582-1405-8

SUBJECT: Family/Identity/Women's Lives
(Fiction)

PRAISE FOR HOLLY CHAMBERLIN AND *THE FRIENDS WE KEEP:*

"A well written and fascinating story."—**Romance Reviews Today**

"Witty, yet quietly introspective."—**Romantic Times**

SUMMARY: In this compelling, heartfelt novel from the bestselling author of *Tuscan Holiday* and *The Friends We Keep*, a family reunited for the holidays explores the price of secrets, the power of regret, and the choices that can change everything. The Rowans' rambling Maine farmhouse is just big enough to contain the family members gathered there in the week before Christmas. Becca Rowan has driven north from Boston with one thought in mind—reclaiming the daughter she gave up when she was a frightened teenager. Raised by Becca's older brother and his wife, Rain Rowan, now sixteen, has no idea she was adopted. Though Becca agreed not to reveal the truth until Rain turned 21, lately that promise, along with all her career success, counts for little in the face of her loneliness and longing. While Becca anticipates shock at her announcement, she's unprepared for the depth of her family's reactions. And as the Rowans' neighbor, Alex, draws her deeper into an unexpected friendship, Becca begins to challenge her own preconceptions about family, love, and the courage needed to live with—and sometimes change—the decisions we make.

ABOUT THE AUTHOR: **Holly Chamberlin** is a native New Yorker, but she now lives in Maine—the aftermath of stumbling across Mr. Right at the one moment she wasn't watching the terrain. She's been writing and editing—poetry, children's fantasies, a romance novel or two, among many other genres and projects—her entire life.

1. Thinking about her husband's affair and about the human appetite for gossip and rumor, Nora posits that "No relationship was entirely private." Do you agree with her assessment?

2. From her vantage point of almost ninety years, Nora believes that "The young thought they were noble, but nobody untested can be noble.... To forgive in the wake of betrayal, that was nobility." Do you agree that nobility—wisdom, wise action, and selfless behavior—comes only (though not necessarily) with age?

3. Discuss Becca's shame and guilt over not having bonded immediately with her baby. How do societal expectations act unfairly on women at various stages of their lives?

4. Lily wonders if it's possible to live a perfectly honest and open life. Is Lily simply naïve, or does her belief in the possibility of a life of honesty hold some merit?

5. Do you believe that some secrets—perhaps the sort found in this novel—should be kept and others broken? Why? In what circumstances?

6. Olivia declares: "Without our memories we're nothing." What does she mean by this? What might a person less obsessed with history understand by this statement?

7. Early on in the novel, Becca reminds herself: "Sentimentality was as dangerous as its troublemaking cohort, nostalgia." Do you agree with her wariness regarding these two emotional states?

8. What do you think of the value of domestic habit in a marriage or other long-term relationship? Do you think it is generally of more importance to a woman than a man, or do you think both sexes equally need and find comfort in domestic habit?

9. Discuss what Alex means when he talks about emotional creativity and its relation to happiness.

10. Becca repeatedly says that she wants to "claim" or "reclaim" her daughter. At one point, Naomi argues against the choice of those terms. She finds them in some way demeaning of Rain's full status as an individual. Do you agree with Naomi's interpretation of Becca's word choice?

11. In your opinion, what is the most important stimulus behind Becca's seemingly abrupt decision to finally talk with her father and begin the healing process between them?

PEOPLE OF THE BOOK

AUTHOR: *Geraldine Brooks*

PUBLISHER: Penguin Books, 2008

WEBSITE: www.penguingroup.com
www.geraldinebrooks.com

AVAILABLE IN:
Trade Paperback, 400 pages, $15.00
ISBN: 978-0143115007

SUBJECT: History/Culture & World Issues/
Art (Fiction)

"Erudite but suspenseful . . . one of the most popular and successful works of fiction in the New Year."—**Alan Cheuse, NPR/"All Things Considered"**

"As full of heart and curiosity as it is intelligence and judgment."
—*The Boston Globe*

SUMMARY: In 1996, Hanna Heath, a young Australian book conservator, has been called to handle the job of a lifetime: analysis of the famed Sarajevo Haggadah, a six hundred year old Jewish prayer book that has been salvaged from the destroyed Bosnian library by a courageous librarian. She discovers a series of artifacts—an insect wing, holes where clasps should have been, wine and salt stains, and a white hair. Hanna investigates these items back to Bosnia during World War II, Vienna in 1894, Venice in 1609, Barcelona in 1492, and Seville in 1480. In vivid detail, we enter the worlds of the people of the book, the Muslim librarian in Sarajevo who saved it from the Nazis; the Venetian ecclesiastical censor who in a fit of rage and personal anguish also protected it from destruction; the sofer, or scribe, who wrote the text; and lastly the mysterious illuminator, whose striking illustrations grace its pages. Hanna's investigation enables her to expose a nefarious international cover up.

ABOUT THE AUTHOR: **Geraldine Brooks** is the author of *Year of Wonders* and the nonfiction works *Nine Parts of Desire* and *Foreign Correspondence*. Previously, Brooks was a correspondent for *The Wall Street Journal*.

1. When Hanna implores Ozren to solicit a second opinion on Alia's condition, he becomes angry and tells her, "Not every story has a happy ending." To what extent do you believe that their perspectives on tragedy and death are cultural? To what extent are they personal?

2. Isak tells Mordechai, "At least the pigeon does no harm. The hawk lives at the expense of other creatures that dwell in the desert." If you were Lola, would you have left the safety of your known life and gone to Palestine? Is it better to live as a pigeon or a hawk? Or is there an alternative?

3. When Father Vistorni asks Rabbi Judah Ayreh to warn the printer that the Church disapproves of one of their recently published texts, Ayreh tells him, "better you do it than to have us so intellectually enslaved that we do it for you." Do you agree or disagree with his argument? With the way he handled Vistorni's request?

4. What was it, ultimately, that made Father Vistorini approve the Haggadah? Since Brooks leaves this part of the story unclear, how do you imagine it made its way from his rooms to Sarajevo?

5. Several of the novel's female characters lived in the pre-feminist era and certainly fared poorly at the hands of men. Does the fact that she was pushing for gender equality—not to mention saving lives—justify Sarah Heath's poor parenting skills? Would women's rights be where they are today if it weren't for women like her?

6. Have you ever been in a position where your professional judgment has been called into question? How did you react?

7. Was Hanna being fair to suspect only Amitai of the theft? Do you think charges should have been pressed against the culprits?

8. How did Hanna change after discovering the truth about her father? Would the person she was before her mother's accident have realized that she loved Ozren? Or risked the dangers involved in returning the codex?

9. There is an amazing array of "people of the book"—both base and noble—whose lifetimes span some remarkable periods in human history. Who is your favorite and why?

THE PIANO TEACHER

AUTHOR: *Janice Y. K. Lee*

PUBLISHER: Penguin Books, 2009

WEBSITE: www.penguingroup.com
www.janiceyklee.com

AVAILABLE IN:
Trade Paperback, 336 pages, $15.00
ISBN: 978-1-440-65625-5

SUBJECT: History/Love & Romance/
Culture & World Issues (Fiction)

"Lee delivers a standout debut. . . . The rippling of past actions through to the present lends the narrative layers of intrigue and more than a few unexpected twists. Lee covers a little- known time in Chinese history without melodrama, and deconstructs without judgment the choices people make in order to live one more day under torturous circumstances."
—***Publishers Weekly***

SUMMARY: In 1942, Will Truesdale, an Englishman newly arrived in Hong Kong, falls headlong into a relationship with Trudy Liang, a beautiful Eurasian socialite. But their love affair is soon threatened by the invasion of the Japanese as World War II. Will is sent to an internment camp, where he and other foreigners struggle daily for survival. Meanwhile, Trudy remains outside, forced to form dangerous alliances with the Japanese. Ten years later, Claire Pendleton comes to Hong Kong and is hired by the wealthy Chen family as their daughter's piano teacher. A provincial English newlywed, Claire is seduced by the heady social life of the expatriate community. She meets Will, to whom she is instantly attracted—but as their affair intensifies, Claire discovers that Will's enigmatic persona hides a devastating past. Long-buried secrets start to emerge and Claire learns that sometimes the price of survival is love.

ABOUT THE AUTHOR: **Janice Y. K. Lee** was born and raised in Hong Kong. She is a former features editor at *Elle* and *Mirabella* magazines in New York. *The Piano Teacher* is her first book.

1. Why does Claire steal from the Chens? Why does she stop doing it?

2. Part of Claire's attraction to Will is that he allows her to be someone different than she had always been. Have you ever been drawn to a person or a situation because it offered you the opportunity to reinvent yourself?

3. The amahs are a steady but silent presence throughout the book. Imagine Trudy and Will's relationship and then Claire and Will's affair from their point of view and discuss

4. Trudy was initially drawn to Will because of his quiet equanimity and Will to Claire because of her innocence. Yet those are precisely the qualities each loses in the course of their love affairs. What does this say about the nature of these relationships? Would Will have been attracted to a woman like Claire before Trudy?

5. What is the irony behind Claire's adoration of the young Princess Elizabeth?

6. Were Dominick and Trudy guilty of collaboration, or were they simply trying to survive? Do their circumstances absolve them of their actions?

7. Mary, Tobias's mother, and one of Will's fellow prisoners in Stanley, does not take advantage of her job in the kitchen to steal more food for her son. Yet she prostitutes herself to preserve him. Is Tobias's physical survival worth the psychological damage she's inflicting?

8. Did Trudy give her emerald ring and Locket to Melody? How much did Melody really know?

9. How do Ned Young's experiences parallel Trudy's?

10. Did Will fail Trudy? Was his decision to remain in Stanley rather than be with her on the outside—as he believes—an act of cowardice?

11. Would Locket be better off knowing the truth about her parentage?

12. What would happen if Trudy somehow survived and came back to Will? Could they find happiness together?

REAL LIFE AND LIARS

AUTHOR: *Kristina Riggle*

PUBLISHER: Avon A, 2009

WEBSITE: www.harpercollins.com
www.kristinariggle.com

AVAILABLE IN:
Trade Paperback, 352 pages, $13.99
ISBN: 978-0-061-70628-8

SUBJECT: Family/Love & Romance/
Personal Discovery (Fiction)

"In her wondrously affecting debut novel Real Life and Liars, *Kristina Riggle accomplished something authors almost never do anymore: she made me care about her characters—and what a wide-ranging cast of characters they are! She made me want good things for them."*—**Lauren Baratz-Logsted, author of** *Baby Needs a New Pair of Shoes*

"A seemingly celebratory gathering brings joy, frustration, love and disappointment to a midwestern family in this wonderful debut novel. These are characters we know and care about from our own lives."
—**Denise Taylor, manager, Schuler Books and Music**

SUMMARY: For Mirabelle Zielinski's children, happiness always seems to be just out of reach. Her polished oldest daughter, Katya, clings to a stale marriage with a workaholic husband and three spoiled children. Her son, Ivan, so creative, is a down-in-the-dumps songwriter with the worst taste in women. And the "baby," impulsive Irina, who lives life on a whim, is now reluctantly pregnant and hitched to a man who is twice her age. On the weekend of their parents' anniversary party, lies will be revealed, hearts will be broken . . . but love will also be found. And the biggest shock may come from Mirabelle herself, because she has a secret that will change everything.

ABOUT THE AUTHOR: **Kristina Riggle** lives and writes in West Michigan. Besides her debut novel, *Real Life & Liars*, she has published short stories in the *Cimarron Review, Literary Mama, Espresso Fiction,* and elsewhere. She is also a freelance journalist writing primarily for *The Grand Rapids Press*, and co-editor for fiction at *Literary Mama*.

1. Does Mira's reluctance to have surgery for her breast cancer seem understandable? What other reasons might she have for this reluctance beyond what she shares directly with the reader in the opening chapter?
2. Which significant life changes are facing Mira, and how might those changes be affecting her state of mind regarding the cancer diagnosis?
3. How would you describe the relationship of Mira to each of her children? How do these relationships affect the plot of the novel?
4. How do you react to Mira's marijuana use? How much does it affect her decision-making throughout the book?
5. How would you describe the marriage of Mira and Max? How do you think their relationship play into her reaction to her cancer diagnosis?
6. How does birth order affect the three grown siblings and how they fit into the family?
7. Which main character—Mira, Katya, Ivan or Irina—do you find most relatable? What parallels can you draw to your own life?
8. Mira observes in the book that children grow up any way they want to, despite a parent's best efforts. Do you agree with this?
9. Why does Katya find herself driving by her old boyfriend's house and calling him secretly? Have you ever felt drawn to a romance from your past?
10. What is the source of the friction between Mira and Katya, and does it seem justified to you? Do you have old childhood fights with your parents that still echo in your adulthood?
11. Do you think Katya and Charles's marriage will endure? Do you think Katya will truly change her life? If so, in what ways?
12. Do you agree with Katya's decision to stay with Charles? How else might she have reacted?
13. Why is Ivan so clueless about romance?
14. Do you think Jenny and Ivan have a future together? Why or why not?
15. Why do you think Irina engages in reckless romantic behavior?
16. What do you think Irina should do about Darius and the baby?
17. Do you believe Mira will change her mind about the surgery when she sees the doctor again? Why or why not?
18. What is the role the Big Tree serves in the novel?
19. How does Mira's lack of formalized religion play into the story? Do you believe her view has changed by the end?
20. How does the setting affect each of the characters?
21. Do you think the Zielinskis are a happy family at the beginning? How about at the end of the novel?

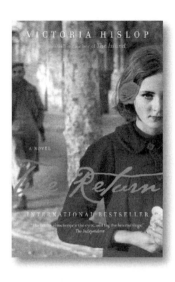

THE RETURN

AUTHOR: *Victoria Hislop*

PUBLISHER: Harper paperbacks,
October 2009

WEBSITE: www.victoriahislop.com
www.harpercollins.com

AVAILABLE IN:
Trade Paperback, 416 pages, $14.99
ISBN: 978-0-06-171541-9

SUBJECT: History/Culture & World Issues/
Relationships (Fiction)

"Hislop uses the same blend of meticulously researched historical narrative and imaginative storytelling that won her plaudits for her first novel, The Island, *to convey this tumultuous time. The rhythms of flamenco resonate on every page and the anguish felt by Concha, the mother of the family . . . brings home the hardships of war in a way no history book ever could."*—Daily Telegraph **(London)**

SUMMARY: From the internationally bestselling author of *The Island* comes a dazzling new novel of family betrayals, forbidden love, and historical turmoil. Sonia knows nothing of the Granada's shocking past, but ordering a simple cup of coffee in a quiet cafe will lead her into the extraordinary tale of a family's fight to survive the horror of the Spanish Civil War. Seventy years earlier, in the Ramirez family's cafe, Concha and Pablo's children relish an atmosphere of hope. Antonio is a serious young teacher, Ignacio a flamboyant matador, and Emilio a skilled musician. Their sister, Mercedes, is a spirited girl whose sole passion is dancing, until she meets Javier and an obsessive love affair begins. But soon Spain is a country in turmoil. In the heat of civil war, the family is torn apart, with the brothers on opposite sides of the conflict and Mercedes trapped on the wrong side of the line, cruelly separated from her beloved Javier. Everyone must take a side, and choose whether to submit, to fight or to attempt escape.

ABOUT THE AUTHOR: **Victoria Hislop**'s first novel, *The Island*, was published in 2006 and won her 'Newcomer of the Year' at the Galaxy British Book Awards 2007. She lives in Sissinghurst with her husband, Ian Hislop, and their two teenage children.

1. "In the picture book of marriage, they were the perfect married couple. It was a story told for an audience." (p.54) What does this extract tell us about Sonia and James's relationship? What changes between them as the novel progresses? Is James a villain? What tactics does he employ to control Sonia?

2. Compare the representations of contemporary Spain and Britain in the book's first two chapters. How do the two countries differ? How does the Britain of 2001 compare with the pre-war version portrayed at the end of the book?

3. Why are music and dance so important to the characters in *The Return*? What does the way a character dances say about them and their relationships?

4. What image of masculinity do the Ramírez males—and the other men in the book—present? How does masculinity differ in Spain and England? Is maleness portrayed as a good or bad thing? How do women exert their power?

5. Did you identify any family traits that ran through the Ramírez generations? Does Sonia take after her father or her mother, or any of her other relations?

6. "For Ignacio, there was a distinction between what he regarded as being a casual informer and actually being an assassin" (p.240). Why does Ignacio make this distinction? Is it an accurate one? Where else in the novel are we invited to compare physical violence with more subtle forms of cruelty?

7. Why does Mercedes lose her faith? How does *The Return* portray religion and particularly the Catholic Church?

8. What does this book have to say about friendship? Is blood thicker than water?

9. What is the role of secrets or non-disclosures? How do they affect the plot?

10. What did you make of Javier and Mercedes' relationship? Is it a childish infatuation, a survival tactic, a "fathomless love" (p.455), or what?

11. Did you detect a political bias to this book? If so, what is it?

12. What is the relevance of bull fighting in *The Return*? Does it tell us anything about Spanish culture or the Civil War more generally?

13. Is Victoria Hislop successful in melding fact and fiction together?

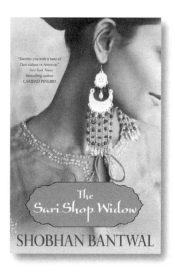

THE SARI SHOP WIDOW

AUTHOR: *Shobhan Bantwal*

PUBLISHER: Kensington Books, 2009

WEBSITE: www.kensingtonbooks.com
www.shobhanbantwal.com

AVAILABLE IN:
Trade Paperback, 352 pages, $16.00
ISBN: 978-0-7582-3202-1

SUBJECT: Women's Lives/Relationships/
Love & Romance (Fiction)

"Dazzles you with a taste of Desi culture in America."—The New York Times **bestselling author Caridad Piñeiro**

SUMMARY: Shobhan Bantwal's compelling new novel is set on the streets of Edison, New Jersey's Little India, where a young businesswoman rediscovers the magic of love and family. Since becoming a widow at age twenty-seven, Anjali Kapadia has devoted herself to transforming her parents' sari shop into a chic boutique. Now, ten years later, it stands out like a proud maharani amid Edison's bustling Little India. But when Anjali learns the shop is on the brink of bankruptcy, she feels her world unraveling. To the rescue comes Anjali's wealthy, dictatorial Uncle Jeevan and his business partner, Rishi Shah—a mysterious Londoner, complete with British accent, cool gray eyes, and skin so fair it makes it hard to believe he's Indian. Rishi's cool, foreign demeanor triggers distrust in Anjali and her mother. But for Anjali, he also stirs something else, a powerful attraction she hasn't felt in a decade. And the feeling is mutual. Love disappointed Anjali once before, and she's vowed to live without it—though Rishi is slowly melting her resolve and as the shop regains its footing, gaining her trust. But when a secret from Rishi's past is revealed, Anjali must turn to her family and her strong cultural upbringing to guide her in finding the truth.

ABOUT THE AUTHOR: **Shobhan Bantwal** was born and raised in India and came to the United States as a young bride in an arranged marriage. She has published short fiction in literary magazines and articles in a number of publications. She lives in New Jersey with her husband. Shobhan loves to hear from her readers. Feel free to e-mail her at shobhan@shobhanbantwal.com.

1. Anjali Kapadia is a Hindu widow from a conservative family. Is her life different compared to the lives of the widows from other cultures? Discuss the uniqueness of her situation.
2. Is a sari and jewelry boutique a good backdrop for the book set in the United States? Could it have been a different background, something that could have given the story an entirely different twist?
3. Jeevan-kaka, Anjali's uncle from India, is an autocratic man with an agenda of his own. Discuss his entry into the lives of Anjali and her family, and the consequences.
4. What role does Anjali's brother Nilesh play in this story? What role does he bring to the plot?
5. Discuss Anjali's lingering feelings for her dead husband and how they influence her actions and emotions throughout the book.
6. Why do you think Anjali has picked an unlikely man like Kip Rowling for a secret boyfriend? What kind of impact does he have on her life and the story?
7. Rishi Shah is the reluctant and unwelcome third party when he is introduced to Anjali. Do you think her overtly hostile reaction to him is justified?
8. What are some of the consequences of a widow falling in love with a man of mixed race, a man who does not even live in the same country?
9. Discuss Rishi's relationship and eventual breakup with his girlfriend, Samantha. Compare and contrast that with Anjali's relationship with Kip.
10. Does the grand opening of the new *Silk & Sapphires* store offer any insights into the planning and running of a large and diverse ethnic business? What about the cultural elements introduced as part of the opening festivities?
11. Jeevan-kaka has a couple of deep secrets, which are revealed toward the end. What do you think of the motives behind his actions, and some of the ramifications of his disclosures?
12. Discuss the unique Hindu family structure as portrayed in this story. How is this domestic arrangement different from that of western cultures? How does it affect Anjali's present life and her potential future with Rishi?
13. Could the story have ended any other way? The author gravitates toward happy or hopeful endings, but you could discuss some other, highly interesting possibilities. And the possibilities are always endless.

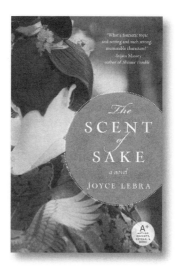

THE SCENT OF SAKE

AUTHOR: *Joyce Lebra*

PUBLISHER: Avon A, 2009

WEBSITE: www.avonbooks.com
        www.joycechapmanlebra.com

AVAILABLE IN:
Trade Paperback, 384 pages, $13.99
ISBN: 978-0-06-166237-9

SUBJECT: History/Personal Triumph/
Women's Lives (Historical Fiction)

"The complex and unusual social norms and mores of nineteenth-century Japan are woven cleanly into the story line, without clumsy exposition. The unfamiliar setting allows Lebra to create a historically believable heroine that modern women can relate to, a difficult task for historical fiction."—Booklist

SUMMARY: She was taught to submit, to obey . . . but she dreamed of an empire. The sole heir to the House of Omura, a venerable family of Kobe sake brewers, nineteen-year-old Rie hears but cannot heed her mother's advice: that in nineteenth-century Japan, a woman must "kill the self" or her life will be too difficult to bear. In this strict, male-dominated society, women may not even enter the brewery—and repressive tradition demands that Rie turn over her family's business to the inept philanderer she's been forced to marry. But Rie's pride will not allow her to relinquish what is rightfully hers. With courage, cunning, brilliance, and skill, she is ready to confront every threat that arises before her—from prejudice to treachery to shipwrecks to the insidious schemes of relentless rivals—in her bold determination to forge a magnificent dynasty . . . and to, impossibly, succeed. An epic and breathtaking saga that spans generations as it sweeps through the heart of a century, Joyce Lebra's *The Scent of Sake* is a vivid and powerful entry into another world . . . and an unforgettable portrait of a woman who would not let that world defeat her.

ABOUT THE AUTHOR: **Joyce Lebra**, a recognized authority on the cultures of Japan, India, and Asia/Pacific women, is professor emerita of Colorado University. She lived in Japan many years and authored 12 nonfiction books.

1. Were you surprised by how powerful sake brewers were in the eighteenth and nineteenth centuries?

2. Why was this house happy to have a daughter as an only child?

3. Was Jihei a typical mukoyoshi, adopted husband/househead?

4. What challenges did Rie face as a woman? What advantages did she have as house daughter?

5. Why was Rie so unhappy to have Yoshitaro adopted as househead and heir? Would you be?

6. Do you think arranged marriages worked at the time?

7. Why were people so surprised Rie wanted to adopt a mukoyoshi for Fumi?

8. Some Americans have asked, why didn't Rie have the nerve to sneak into the kura when no one was looking? What do you think?

9. What would have happened had Rie been discovered during her assignation with Saburo? What would have happened to Saburo?

10. What was your reaction when Rie demanded that Kinno divorce Nobu?

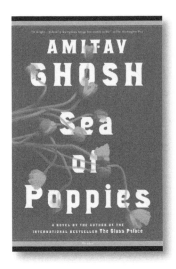

SEA OF POPPIES

AUTHOR: *Amitav Ghosh*

PUBLISHER: Picador USA, 2009

WEBSITE: us.macmillan.com/seaofpoppies
www.amitavghosh.com

AVAILABLE IN:
Trade Paperback, 528 pages, $15.00
ISBN: 978-0-312-42859-4

SUBJECT: History/Adventure/Culture &
World Issues (Fiction)

"Any reader would be forgiven, upon finishing the Indian writer Amitav Ghosh's new novel Sea of Poppies, *for suspecting that Ghosh is an avatar of Charles Dickens."*—**Art Winslow, Chicago Tribune**

SUMMARY: At the heart of this vibrant saga is a vast ship, the *Ibis*. Its destiny is a tumultuous voyage across the Indian Ocean; its purpose, to fight China's vicious nineteenth-century Opium Wars. As for the crew, they are a motley array of sailors and stowaways, coolies and convicts.

In a time of colonial upheaval, fate has thrown together a diverse cast of Indians and Westerners, from a bankrupt raja to a widowed tribeswoman, from a mulatto American freedman to a freespirited French orphan. They, like their historical counterparts, come to view themselves as *jahaj-bhais*, or ship-brothers. An unlikely dynasty is born, which will span continents, races, and generations.

The vast sweep of this historical adventure spans the lush poppy fields of the Ganges, the rolling high seas, the exotic backstreets of Canton. But it is the panorama of characters, whose diaspora encapsulates the vexed colonial history of the East itself, that makes *Sea of Poppies* so breathtakingly alive—a masterpiece from one of the world's finest novelists.

ABOUT THE AUTHOR: **Amitav Ghosh** is the internationally bestselling author of many works of fiction and nonfiction, including *The Glass Palace*. Ghosh divides his time between Kolkata and Goa, India, and Brooklyn, New York.

1. Discuss how the relationships between the various classes of people aboard the *Ibis* change throughout the novel. To what extent does the caste system affect these relationships? Which characters undergo the most significant changes?

2. How are women's roles different from men's in *Sea of Poppies*? What common ground do Deeti, Paulette, and Munia share?

3. What does the *Ibis* represent to Zachary at various points in the novel? How does his perception of the ship change as his perception of himself changes?

4. Many of the lives Ghosh depicts are shaped by social and political forces beyond their control. What are some of these forces? Describe some of the individual acts of bravery, defiance, or deception that enable his characters to break free from what they see as their fate.

5. How do those involved in the opium trade justify their work in *Sea of Poppies*? How does their industry compare to modern-day drug trafficking versus the pharmaceutical industry?

6. When Mr. Burnham gives religious instruction to Paulette, what does he reveal about his mindset in general? How does he balance his shame with his attitudes toward suffering, including his notion that slavery somehow yields freedom?

7. Discuss the power of love as it motivates the characters. Does obsession strengthen or weaken Baboo Nob Kissin? What kind of love is illustrated when Deeti gives up her child? What kinds of love does Neel experience in the presence of his loyal wife and his fickle mistress?

8. How did Paulette's free-spirited upbringing serve her later in life? What advantages and disadvantages did she have?

9. What does Zachary teach Jodu about loyalty and survival? How is trust formed among the suspicious *Ibis* crew?

10. Which historical aspects of the Opium Wars surprised you the most? What did you discover about colonial India by reading *Sea of Poppies*?

11. *Sea of Poppies* makes rich use of Asian-influenced English. Some of the words, such as *bandanna, loot, and dinghy*, are still used frequently, but many others, like *bankshall, wanderoo, and chawbuck*, are now rare. Discuss the *Ibis* Chrestomathy, which appears at the end of the book. Can a culture's vitality be measured by how eagerly its language absorbs outside influences?

12. How does *Sea of Poppies* reflect themes you have observed in Amitav Ghosh's previous works? What new issues does he explore in this novel?

THE SEAMSTRESS

AUTHOR: *Frances de Pontes Peebles*

PUBLISHER: Harper Perennial, 2009

WEBSITE: www.harperperennial.com
www.francesdepontespeebles.com

AVAILABLE IN:
Trade Paperback, 656 pages, $15.99
ISBN: 978-0-060-73888-4

SUBJECT: Family/Culture & World Issues/
Adventure (Fiction)

"[A] richly woven tale. . . . This is the best book I've read in the past year. . . . This saga of motherless sisters unfolds against a panoramic backdrop of drought and political unrest. . . . Fans of Isabel Allende will find much to recommend in this saga, with its fully realized characters, gripping moral quandries, tense drama, and lyrical descriptive prose."—Elle

SUMMARY: As seamstresses, the young sisters Emília and Luzia dos Santos know how to cut, how to mend, and how to conceal. These are useful skills in the lawless backcountry of Brazil, where ruthless land barons called "colonels" feud with bands of outlaw cangaceiros, trapping innocent residents in the cross fire. But when Luzia is abducted by a group of cangaceiros led by the infamous Hawk, the sisters' quiet lives diverge in ways they never imagined. Emília stumbles into marriage with Degas Coelho, the son of a doctor whose wealth is rivaled only by his political power. Luzia, forced to trek through scrubland and endure a nomadic existence, proves her determination to survive and begins to see the cangaceiros as comrades, not criminals. But Luzia will overcome time and distance to entrust her sister with a great secret—one Emília vows to keep. And when Luzia's life is threatened, Emília will risk everything to save her. *The Seamstress* is impeccably drawn, rich in depth and vision, and heralds the arrival of a supremely talented new writer.

ABOUT THE AUTHOR: **Frances de Pontes Peebles** was born in Pernambuco, Brazil and raised in Miami, Florida. Her short stories have appeared in *Zoetrope: All-Story*, the *Indiana Review*, the *Missouri Review*, and the *O. Henry Prize Story Collection 2005*.

1. How does their shared childhood as poor, religious, orphaned seamstresses shape Emília and Luzia's unique perspectives on life?

2. How does access to water define political power in a country like Brazil in the 1920s and 1930s? How did the author's descriptions of extreme drought affect your appreciation of modern conveniences?

3. How does the Hawk's treatment of Luzia in the caatinga, or scrub, reveal Antônio's true nature?

4. What does Emília's reception into Recife society indicate about the esteem in which the Coelho family is held? To what extent is her mother-in-law, Dona Dulce Coelho, overly concerned about others' perceptions of Emília?

5. To what extent are secrets responsible for the marriage between Degas and Emília and, much later, for its disintegration?

6. How does Luzia's behavior in the initial aftermath of Antônio's death explain her success in becoming the new captain of the cangaceiros? In what other ways does her behavior change once the Hawk is dead?

7. How do Dr. Duarte's interests in phrenology and politics and his import-export business connect him to the government's search for The Seamstress and the Hawk?

8. At various points in the novel, how does Dr. Eronildes Epifano represent both salvation and damnation to the cangaceiros? What role does Degas play in alerting Emília to Dr. Eronildes's duplicity?

9. Given The Seamstress's attacks on innocent people, to what extent are Emília's efforts to communicate information to Luzia through newspaper articles and photographs ethically defensible?

10. How does the book's final image connect with earlier images of bones in *The Seamstress*? Why do you think the author chose to close her book with this image?

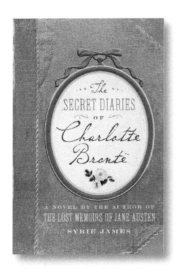

THE SECRET DIARIES OF CHARLOTTE BRONTË

AUTHOR: *Syrie James*

PUBLISHER: Avon A, 2009

WEBSITE: www.harpercollins.com
www.syriejames.com

AVAILABLE IN:
Trade Paperback, 512 pages, $14.99
ISBN: 978-0-061-64837-3

SUBJECT: History/Family/Women's Lives
(Historical Fiction)

SUMMARY: "I have written about the joys of love. I have, in my secret heart, long dreamt of an intimate connection with a man; every Jane, I believe, deserves her Rochester." Though poor, plain, and unconnected, Charlotte Brontë possesses a deeply passionate side which she reveals only in her writings—creating *Jane Eyre* and other novels that stand among literature's most beloved works. Living a secluded life in the wilds of Yorkshire, Charlotte Brontë dreams of a real love story as fiery as the ones she creates. But it is in the pages of her diary where Charlotte exposes her deepest feelings and desires—and the truth about her life, its triumphs and shattering disappointments, her family, the inspiration behind her work, her scandalous secret passion for the man she can never have . . . and her intense, dramatic relationship with the man she comes to love, the enigmatic Arthur Bell Nicholls.

From Syrie James, the acclaimed, bestselling author of *The Lost Memoirs of Jane Austen*, comes a powerfully compelling, intensely researched literary feat that blends historical fact and fiction to explore the passionate heart and unquiet soul of Charlotte Brontë. It is Charlotte's story, just as she might have written it herself.

ABOUT THE AUTHOR: **Syrie James** is a scholar of 19th-century British literature and a long-time admirer of Jane Austen's work. *The Lost Memoirs of Jane Austen* was her first work of historical fiction.

1. Describe Charlotte's relationship with her sisters, Emily and Anne. How did her relationship with her brother Branwell evolve and change over the years, and what influence did he have on her life?

2. What secrets did Charlotte and her siblings each keep, and why? Whose secret had the most devastating impact on the family? How did Charlotte's secret affect her life and her work?

3. Who are your favorite characters in the novel, and why? Who is your least favorite character?

4. What are your favorite scenes in the novel? What was the saddest scene? The happiest? The most uplifting? Did any scene make you laugh or cry?

5. Did hearing the story of Charlotte's life in the first person enhance the reading experience for you? What are the benefits of telling this story from the main character's perspective, rather than the third person? What are the limitations?

6. Why were Emily and Charlotte both so insistent on keeping their writing ambitions a secret? Why did they choose an androgynous pseudonym? Once published, how did the reality compare to the dream for each of them? How did Charlotte's life change when she was no longer able to "walk invisible"?

7. Would you consider Charlotte a feminist in today's terms? Do you think Charlotte's views affected her feelings about marriage?

8. Strict laws at the time gave a husband ownership of his wife's body, her property and wages, and custody of their children. Discuss other conditions in Victorian England, with regard to women—i.e., health, sanitation, food, travel, career opportunities, courtship, sex, and conventions of feminine beauty. How did they differ from our lives today? In what ways are things still the same?

9. Examine the many ways in which Charlotte dramatized her own life experiences in her novels. How many people, places and events from her real life can you identify in Jane Eyre? Shirley? Villette?

10. Compare and contrast Charlotte Brontë and her fictional creation, Jane Eyre, in terms of physical appearance, personality, romantic sensibilities and psychological desires.

11. How successfully does the author capture Charlotte Brontë's voice? Did the novel inspire you to read or reread Charlotte's works, or the works of her sisters?

THE SECRET PAPERS OF MADAME OLIVETTI

AUTHOR: *Annie Vanderbilt*

PUBLISHER: New American Library, 2008

WEBSITE: www.penguingroup.com
www.annievanderbilt.com

AVAILABLE IN:
Trade Paperback, 304 pages, $15.00
ISBN: 978-0-451-22527-6

SUBJECT: Women's Lives/Relationships/
Love & Romance (Fiction)

"I thoroughly enjoyed this wise, witty, sensuous exploration of a woman looking back over her rich and complex life."—**Lisa Tucker, national bestselling author of *Once Upon a Day* and *The Cure for Modern Life***

"In [her] sensuous and scenic debut novel . . . Vanderbilt carefully paints a stunning portrait of love in its many forms."—***Booklist***

SUMMARY: Lily has come to southern France in search of a new perspective, hoping that the sun's soft rays and the fragrant sea breezes will provide a relaxing respite from the demands of her lively daughter and her family's Idaho cattle ranch. Two years after her husband's sudden death, in the house that has been in his family for generations, she finally finds some stolen weeks to make sense of the past. To Madame Olivetti—her cranky old manual typewriter—Lily entrusts all her secrets, pounding out the story of the men she loved, the betrayals she endured, the losses she still regrets. And with the companionship of Yves, the seductive handyman who comes by to make repairs, Lily comes closer to understanding her exhilarating past—and to discovering she has a new story to tell—one about the delights of starting over.

ABOUT THE AUTHOR: **Annie Vanderbilt** graduated from Radcliffe College and has been a Peace Corps volunteer in India, a leader of wilderness programs for high school students, co-owner of a ski touring center in Idaho, and a 'round the world bicyclist and backpacker. She lives with her husband on an island in Florida and in the mountains of Idaho.

1. Why does Lily choose to reveal her lifetime of secrets to a typewriter and a French handyman who can't understand a word she says because he speaks no English?

2. Do you think that Lily's sexuality is a detriment, or does it add to her inner strength and ability to deal with life's reversals?

3. What character traits in Lily and circumstances in her life make it possible for her to move beyond anger, forgive Phila and continue loving her sister? Would you have done the same?

4. Lily says to Paul, "Don't you think it's time the train moved on? For both of us?" What experiences and discoveries help Lily become "unstuck" from her own windows of grief and remorse?

5. Lily finds the women in Paul's family fascinating. The author weaves their romantic and sexual histories into Lily's own story. Why do you think the author has placed Lily in the context of these previous generations of French women?

6. When Lily drives off in Paul's truck, hurt and angry because once again he has let her down, she says to herself, "Welcome to the Club of Disappointment and then count your blessings." What does she mean by this? Does Lily's approach resonate in any way with your own experience of working through the difficult times in a long-term relationship?

7. What losses and disappointments build to the point that Lily betrays Paul? Is her emotional vulnerability in Chiapas understandable?

8. Do you think that Paul knows about Lily's love affair with Victor? If so, why does he choose not to confront her? Does he accept equal responsibility for the breakdown in their marriage? Where else in the book does Paul confront difficult truths about Lily? Does he always do so with equanimity?

9. What is Alonso's role in Lily's story other than that of the neighbor's cat?

10. The author moves back and forth between present and past. What are some of the devices and signposts she uses to make these time shifts flow smoothly?

11. On p. 111 Lily reflects: "Change had not happened to Lily; she had simply introduced new patterns and colors into the weave of her destiny. On p. 135 Justine Lafond says: "I think life is a pack of cards, Lily. When you turn them over they become your history. Until then they are shadows. Shadow cards." Are there other passages in the book that touch on universal themes and make you say *yes, aha, I've been there?*

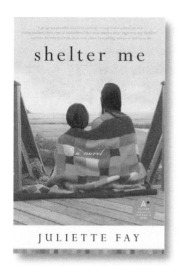

SHELTER ME

AUTHOR: *Juliette Fay*

PUBLISHER: Avon A, 2008

WEBSITE: www.avonbooks.com

AVAILABLE IN:
Trade Paperback, 488 pages, $14.99
ISBN: 978-0-06-167339-9

SUBJECT: Relationships/Identity/Personal Discovery (Fiction)

"A gorgeous paradox of a book: a deep, thoughtful exploration of a young mother's first year of widowhood that is as much a page-turner as any thriller."—**Marisa de los Santos,** *The New York Times* **bestselling author of** *Belong to Me* **and** *Love Walked In*

SUMMARY: In the tradition of Marisa de los Santos and Anne Tyler comes a moving debut about a young mother's year of heartbreak, loss, and forgiveness . . . and help that arrives from unexpected sources. Four months after her husband's death, Janie LaMarche remains undone by grief and anger. Her mourning is disrupted, however, by the unexpected arrival of a builder with a contract to add a porch onto her house. Stunned, Janie realizes the porch was meant to be a surprise from her husband—now his last gift to her. As she reluctantly allows construction to begin, Janie clings to the familiar outposts of her sorrow—mothering her two small children with fierce protectiveness, avoiding friends and family, and stewing in a rage she can't release. Yet Janie's self-imposed isolation is breached by a cast of unlikely interventionists: her chattering aunt; her bossy neighbor; her muffin-bearing cousin; and even Tug, the contractor with a private grief all his own. As the porch takes shape, Janie discovers that the unknowable terrain of the future is best navigated with the help of others—even those we least expect to call on, much less learn to love.

ABOUT THE AUTHOR: **Juliette Fay** received a bachelor's degree from Boston College and a master's degree from Harvard University. She lives in Massachusetts with her husband and four young children. *Shelter Me* is her first novel.

1. The theme of shelter, both literal and figurative, arises again and again throughout the course of the story. Who shelters whom? Are all the instances of "sheltering" helpful, or are some misguided?

2. Janie's mother, the person whom she expects can help the most, is unable or unwilling to be there for her. Meanwhile, the people who offer the greatest support are often people Janie doesn't even like at first. Are her instincts just off, or is life sometimes that surprising?

3. To varying degrees, Janie feels abandoned by a number of people in her life: her husband for dying, her mother for staying away, her neighbor Shelly for moving, and Father Jake for discontinuing their relationship. Are these real betrayals? How do they pulsate with the support she experiences from unexpected sources?

4. Janie becomes acquainted with several people who have experienced sexual abuse (Katya in the self-defense course, Father Jake, and Beryl the homeless woman). How do each of these people and their experiences affect Janie?

5. Did Janie's mother, Noreen, do the right thing by going to Father Jake and asking him to end their relationship? If not, was her action forgivable? What would have happened if she had gone to Janie instead? Did her letter to Janie sufficiently explain her rationale or not? Does Janie ever fully forgive her mother?

6. Janie's husband Robby was the love of her life. How is it, then, that she could fall for two other men within one year of his death? Is it possible to have more than one love of your life? If Father Jake had been willing to leave the priesthood, would they have been happy together?

7. The story has several "travelers": Janie's mother, Beryl the homeless woman, and even Janie's daughter, Carly, seems to be destined for flight. Beryl claims that Janie is, too. In what ways might that be true or not?

8. How might this story have been different if Janie hadn't had children? What various meanings might Dylan's goggles represent?

9. The skills that Janie learns in the self-defense course end up coming in very handy. Besides self-defense, are there other lessons she uses throughout the story?

10. Janie spends a lot of time both asking for and granting forgiveness. How does this alter the course of her relationships? (And can cake really solve interpersonal strife? Might a massive baking effort be the answer to the world's current morass of aggression and destruction?)

11. What happens next? Do Tug and Janie stay together? If so, which "shelter" do they choose to live in—his or hers?

12. If there were a movie based on this story, how would you cast it?

SING THEM HOME

AUTHOR: *Stephanie Kallos*

PUBLISHER: Atlantic Monthly Press, 2009

WEBSITE: www.groveatlantic.com
www.stephaniekallos.com

AVAILABLE IN:
Hardcover, 560 pages, $24.00
ISBN: 978-0-87113-963-4

SUBJECT: Family/Relationships/Identity
(Fiction)

"Fans of Ann Patchett and Haven Kimmel should dive onto the sofa one wintry weekend with Stephanie Kallos's wonderfully transportive second novel, Sing Them Home.*"*—**Karen Valby,** *Entertainment Weekly* **(A-)**

SUMMARY: *Sing Them Home* is a moving portrait of three siblings who have lived in the shadow of unresolved grief since their mother's disappearance when they were children. Everyone in Emlyn Springs knows the story of Hope Jones, the physician's wife whose big dreams for their tiny town were lost along with her in the tornado of 1978. For Hope's three young children, the stability of life with their father, and with Viney, their mother's spitfire best friend, is no match for Hope's absence. Larken, the eldest, is now an art history professor who seeks in food an answer to a less tangible hunger; Gaelan, the son, is a telegenic weatherman who devotes his life to predicting the unpredictable; and the youngest, Bonnie, combs roadsides for clues to her mother's legacy, and permission to move on. After their father's death, each sibling is forced to revisit the childhood tragedy that has defined their lives.

Kallos explores the consequences of protecting those we love. *Sing Them Home* is a magnificent tapestry of lives connected and undone by tragedy, lives poised—unbeknownst to the characters—for redemption.

ABOUT THE AUTHOR: **Stephanie Kallos** is the author of the best-selling, award-winning novel, *Broken for You*, which has been translated into ten languages.

1. Tornados frame this whirlwind of a book, those of 1978 and 2004 in Nebraska. How are these events both apocalyptic and miraculous?
2. What does the title mean? How is the Welsh singing a lifeline for Emlyn Springs? Are music and tornados linked in some kind of magic realism?
3. After she is miraculously rescued, still on her bicycle seat, Bonnie believes she has seen her mother swirled into the atmosphere into the arms of an angel. "The event shaped Bonnie Jones to believe in the improbable, that's sure, and in magic." Is Bonnie's oblique angle on life a curse or a gift for her?
4. "In Emlyn Springs, no one is said to be truly dead until they've been sung to in this manner," in chorus, in shifts, for seventy-two hours. Is this a stunningly appropriate ceremony for the passing of a human life?
5. Another natural disaster is the lightning bolt that strikes Llewellyn down. Do you accept Viney's theory that he was complicit in his own death? That he was bringing a judgment on himself?
6. What are some of the interpolated stories that might at first seem diversions but actually give insight into central concerns of the book?
7. Both Gaelan and Larken achieve success in their careers. How do both suffer humiliation and debacle?
8. What can we say about the nature of friendship in the book? Hope and Viney? Larken and Jon and Esme? Bonnie and Blind Tom? Others? What is suggested about relationships that begin in friendship and end in romance?
9. Were you surprised by the Hope that emerged in her diary? Does this Hope seem different from what you expected?
10. As neurotic and demon-driven as the three siblings are, how are they also sublimely human and happily inconsistent?
11. Is there hope at the end for the three driven characters, Larken, Gaelan, and Bonnie? Any sense of liberation from their demons?
12. In this Nebraska town, people are identified by the quality of their voices, their singing parts, bass, alto, tenor, soprano. Does it seem a protective atmosphere or a claustrophobic one?
13. What purpose do symbols serve in the lives of these characters? Do you have any personal symbols in your own life?
14. How do signs, whether literal or metaphorical, influence the lives of the main characters, particularly Bonnie and Larken? Are you a person who looks for signs when making significant decisions? What "signs" have you encountered in your own life?

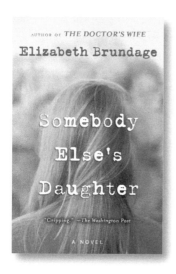

SOMEBODY ELSE'S DAUGHTER

AUTHOR: *Elizabeth Brundage*

PUBLISHER: Plume Books, 2009

WEBSITE: ww.somebodyelsesdaughter.com
www.elizabethbrundage.com

AVAILABLE IN:
Trade Paperback, 352 pages, $15.00
ISBN: 978-0-452-29537-7

SUBJECT: Family/Women Lives/
Social Issues (Fiction)

"[A] deft balancing act of taut plot and richly drawn characters. . . . Brundage is a storyteller supreme."—**Wally Lamb**

"A taut tale of suspense rounded out with sharp observations on parenting, adoption and the fraught business of keeping up appearances."
—**The New York Observer**

SUMMARY: Like *The Doctor's Wife*—which *The Boston Globe* called "a compelling read"—*Somebody Else's Daughter* is a literary page-turner peopled with fascinating and disturbing characters. In the idyllic Berkshires, at the prestigious Pioneer School, there are dark secrets that threaten to come to light. Willa Golding, a student, has been brought up by her adoptive parents in elegant prosperity, but they have fled a mysterious and shameful past. Her biological father, a failing writer and former drug addict, needs to see the daughter he abandoned, and so he gains a teaching position at the school. A feminist sculptor initiates a reckless affair, the Pioneer students live in a world to which adults turn a blind eye, and the headmaster's wife is busy keeping her husband's current indiscretions well hidden. Building to a breathtaking collision between two fathers—biological and adoptive, past and present—*Somebody Else's Daughter* is both a suspenseful thriller and a probing study of richly conflicted characters in emotional turmoil.

ABOUT THE AUTHOR: **Elizabeth Brundage** is the author of *The Doctor's Wife* and holds an MFA in fiction from the Iowa Writers' Workshop. Her short fiction has been published in the *Greensboro Review, Witness magazine*, and *New Letters*. She lives with her family in upstate New York.

1. Many of the book's characters mirror each other—Jack vs. Joe as unfaithful husbands; Joe and Claire, who both use sex as a commodity; Pearl and Willa, the orphaned daughters; Maggie and Candace, the wronged wives. Why does the author choose to use this device? What do we learn about the characters by comparing and contrasting their similarities and differences?

2. Joe defends his work in pornography saying he is simply making a living. How do you feel about pornography? Is his position defensible?

3. Why is Maggie so cowed by Jack? Why does she continue to help him cover up his crimes? Is she a victim of circumstance or of her own actions?

4. A feminist theme runs throughout the book. How do you feel about the author's depictions of feminism? Do today's young women need or care about equality of the sexes? Is feminism still relevant in today's society?

5. The book's title could refer to any or all of the book's female characters. Why do you think the author chose this title?

6. During Candace's meeting with Nate, she refers to Willa's biological parents as indigents. He responds, "We're told certain things, information that pushes us into tidy categories, but they're just words. We're rarely told the whole story and the story is always changing." Considering Candace's checkered past, is it fair of her to stereotype him?

7. Claire is drawn to Nate and Joe, two very different men, who are, respectively, Willa's biological and adoptive fathers. Why did the author choose to connect the men via both Claire and Willa?

8. Jack is clearly the story's villain, yet the author attempts to explain his actions by revealing details about his traumatic childhood. Do these passages make you feel sympathetic toward him?

9. How do you feel about the book's conclusion?

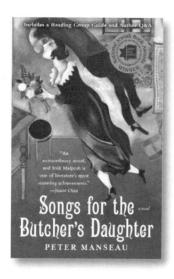

SONGS FOR THE BUTCHER'S DAUGHTER

AUTHOR: *Peter Manseau*

PUBLISHER: Free Press, 2009

WEBSITE: www.simonandschuster.com
www.petermanseau.com

AVAILABLE IN:
Trade Paperback, 400 pages, $14.00
ISBN: 978-1-416-53871-4

SUBJECT: Family/Relationships/Identity (Fiction)

"Songs for the Butcher's Daughter *explores with profound insight the treacherous territory of language: its elusive, inconstant and enigmatic character and its fundamental role in how we define ourselves as human beings."*—**Linda Olsson, author of** *Astrid and Veronika*

SUMMARY: Itsik Malpesh was born the son of a goose-plucking factory manager during the Russian pogroms—his life saved on the night it began by the young daughter of a kosher slaughterer. Or so he believes . . .

Exiled during the war, Itsik eventually finds himself in New York, working as a typesetter and writing poetry to his muse, the butcher's daughter, whom he is sure he will never see again. But it is here in New York that Itsik is unexpectedly reunited with his greatest love—and, later, his greatest enemy—with results both serendipitous and tragic. His story is recounted in his memoirs thanks to the most unlikely of translators—a twenty-one-year-old Boston Catholic college student who, in meeting Itsik, has embarked upon a great lie that will define his future and the most extraordinary friendship he'll ever know.

ABOUT THE AUTHOR: **Peter Manseau** is the author of *Vows* and coauthor of *Killing the Buddha*. He is the editor of *Search, The Magazine of Science, Religion, and Culture*. He lives with his wife and two daughters in Washington, D.C., where he studies religion and teaches writing at Georgetown University.

1. To what extent does the translator's involvement with Malpesh seem grounded in his own preoccupations and emotional needs, rather than in an exact rendering of those of his subject?
2. How would you characterize Sasha Bimko's role in the birth of Itsik Malpesh? How does Malpesh's account of his birth compare to the reality that Sasha discloses to him as an adult? What does his own romanticized vision of his entry into the world reveal about Malpesh's personality? Why does the translator decide to include both accounts of Malpesh's birth in his translated memoir, despite their contradictions?
3. How does the translator's decision to conceal his true religious identity as a Catholic affect his interactions with his coworker, Clara, and with Itsik Malpesh, the subject of his translation? What does his decision to feign being Jewish reveal about his own comfort with his actual identity?
4. How does Itsik's deception of his family in order to learn how to read Russian compare to his translator's deception of his employers to learn Yiddish? How does each man's discovery of a new language open up new worlds to him, and what do these worlds represent in terms of future possibilities, hopes, and dreams?
5. How does the series of translator's notes that appears in the narrative of the *Songs for the Butcher's Daughter* affect your reading of the life story of Itsik Malpesh? To what extent can you imagine this novel stripped of the translator and his story?
6. How does his idealized vision of Sasha Bimko as his destiny, his beloved, and his muse enable Itsik Malpesh to focus his budding ambitions as a poet? To what extent does their eventual romantic involvement seem inevitable, and why does the resolution of that relationship in *Songs for the Butcher's Daughter*, draw in Malpesh's translator and his girlfriend, Clara?
7. What role do their religious differences of opinion play in Malpesh's inability to comprehend Shveig's innocence?
8. How do the translator and Malpesh seem fated for each other? How does the translator's connection to Sasha Bimko, through his relationship with Clara, lead Malpesh back to his bashert?
9. Did you feel that either narratives were more engrossing, or did both engage you equally as a reader? To what extent are these dual narratives able to be separated from each other, and what argument might the author be making about the nature of translation in their interconnectedness?

Peter Manseau is available to speak by phone to reading groups.
Please contact Andy Dodds—Andrew.Dodds@simonandschuster.com.

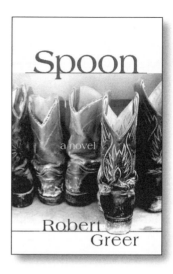

SPOON

AUTHOR: *Robert Greer*

PUBLISHER: Fulcrum Publishing, October 2009

WEBSITE: www.fulcrum-books.com
www.robertgreerbooks.com

AVAILABLE IN:
Hardcover, 256 pages, $24.95
ISBN: 978-1-55591-689-3

SUBJECT: Adventure/Family/Relationships (Fiction)

PRAISE FOR ROBERT GREER

"Greer relaxes into a lean, loose style that fits his Western mysteries like a beat-up pair of lizard-skin boots."—**The New York Times Book Review**

"Robert Greer's writing becomes more powerful with each novel."—**Washington Times**

SUMMARY: A novel of the contemporary American West, *Spoon* tells the story of Arcus Witherspoon, a mysterious half-black, half-Indian, oddly clairvoyant man searching the West for his roots. Hitchhiking near Hardin, Montana, Spoon falls in with a ranching family struggling to keep their ranch afloat amidst the pressures of hard economic times and an encroaching coal company. Proving himself a gifted ranch hand and mentor, Spoon charges himself with rescuing the Darleys and guiding the family's teenage son TJ on his path to manhood. While Spoon's checkered past includes a prison stint and a navy tour of Vietnam, it is his tenacity, wisdom, and charm that end up defining this quintessential Western man.

ABOUT THE AUTHOR: **Robert Greer** is author of the CJ Floyd mystery series: *The Devil's Hatband, The Devil's Red Nickel, The Devil's Backbone, Resurrecting Langston Blue, The Fourth Perspective, The Mongoose Deception, Blackbird, Farewell*, and two medical thrillers. He is a practicing pathologist and professor of medicine at the University of Colorado, and he owns and operates a working cattle ranch in Wyoming.

1. Is there a particular event or scene that influenced the outcome of the book more than another?

2. How do you feel about Spoon as a person? Would you be friends with him? Do you think he's clairvoyant?

3. How much does history affect each of the characters and their relationships with one another?

4. In what ways is *Spoon* a traditional Western? Are there ways in which it challenges this genre classification?

5. What was unique about the setting and how did it enhance or take away from the story?

6. What specific themes did the author emphasize throughout the novel? What do you think he is trying to get across to the reader?

7. Do the characters seem real and believable? Can you relate to their predicaments? To what extent do they remind you of yourself or someone you know?

8. How do characters change or evolve throughout the course of the story? What events trigger such changes?

9. Did certain parts of the book make you uncomfortable? If so, why did you feel that way? Did this lead to a new understanding or awareness of some aspect of your life you might not have thought about before?

10. In what ways did you identify with the situations and/or characters?

11. What major emotions did the story evoke in you as a reader?

12. Many of the ranch owners and families agree that they would die for their land. To what extent does concern for land/property continue today? What would you die for?

STILL ALICE

AUTHOR: *Lisa Genova*

PUBLISHER: Pocket Books, 2009

WEBSITE: www.simonsays.com
www.StillAlice.com

AVAILABLE IN:
Trade Paperback, 320 pages, $15.00
ISBN: 978-1-4391-0281-7

SUBJECT: Family/Relationships/Identity
(Fiction)

"Heartbreakingly real. . . . So real, in fact, that it kept me from sleeping for several nights. I couldn't put it down. . . . Still Alice is a story that must be told."—**Brunonia Barry, *The New York Times* bestselling author of *The Lace Reader***

"After I read Still Alice, *I wanted to stand up and tell a train full of strangers, 'You have to get this book.'"*—**Beverly Beckham, *The Boston Globe***

SUMMARY: *Still Alice* is a compelling debut novel about a 50-year-old woman's sudden descent into early onset Alzheimer's disease. Alice Howland, happily married with three grown children and a house on the Cape, is a celebrated Harvard professor at the height of her career when she notices a forgetfulness creeping into her life. As confusion starts to cloud her thinking and her memory begins to fail her, she receives a devastating diagnosis: early onset Alzheimer's disease. Fiercely independent, Alice struggles to maintain her lifestyle and live in the moment, even as her sense of self is being stripped away. In turns heartbreaking, inspiring and terrifying, *Still Alice* captures in remarkable detail what's it's like to literally lose your mind...

Reminiscent of *A Beautiful Mind, Ordinary People* and *The Curious Incident of the Dog in the Night-time, Still Alice* packs a powerful emotional punch and marks the arrival of a strong new voice in fiction.

ABOUT THE AUTHOR: **Lisa Genova**, a first-time novelist, holds a Ph.D. in neuroscience from Harvard University and is an online columnist for the National Alzheimer's Association. She lives with her family in Massachusetts.

1. After first learning she has Alzheimer's disease, "the sound of her name penetrated her every cell and seemed to scatter her molecules beyond the boundaries of her own skin. She watched herself from the far corner of the room". What do you think of Alice's reaction to the diagnosis? Why does she disassociate herself to the extent that she feels she's having an out-of-body experience?

2. Do you find irony in the fact that Alice, a Harvard professor and researcher, suffers from a disease that causes her brain to atrophy? Why do you think the author, Lisa Genova, chose this profession? How does her past academic success affect Alice's ability, and her family's, to cope with Alzheimer's?

3. When Alice's three children find out they can be tested for the genetic mutation that causes Alzheimer's, only Lydia decides she doesn't want to know. Why does she decline? Would you want to know if you had the gene?

4. Why is her mother's butterfly necklace so important to Alice? Is it only because she misses her mother? Does Alice feel a connection to butterflies beyond the necklace?

5. Alice decides she wants to spend her remaining time with her family and her books. Why doesn't her research make the list of priorities? Does Alice most identify herself as a mother, wife, or scholar?

6. Were you surprised at Alice's plan to overdose on sleeping pills once her disease progressed to an advanced stage? Why does she make this difficult choice? If they found out, would her family approve?

7. Do Alice's relationships with her children differ? Why does she read Lydia's diary? Does Lydia decide to attend college only to honor her mother?

8. Alice and the members of her support group, Mary, Cathy, and Dan, all discuss how their reputations suffered prior to their diagnoses, because people thought they were being difficult or possibly had substance abuse problems. Is preserving their legacies one of the biggest obstacles to people suffering from Alzheimer's disease? What examples are there of people still respecting Alice's wishes, and at what times is she ignored?

9. Why does Lisa Genova choose to end the novel with John reading that Amylex, the medicine that Alice was taking, failed to stabilize Alzheimer's patients? Why does this news cause John to cry?

10. As Alice's disease worsens, her perceptions get less reliable. Why would the author choose to stay in Alice's perspective? What do we gain, and what do we lose?

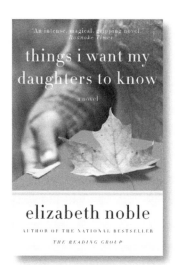

THINGS I WANT MY DAUGHTERS TO KNOW

AUTHOR: *Elizabeth Noble*

PUBLISHER: Harper paperbacks, 2009

WEBSITE: www.elizabethnoblebooks.com
www.harpercollins.com

AVAILABLE IN:
Trade Paperback, 400 pages, $14.99
ISBN: 978-0-061-68659-7

SUBJECT: Family/Relationships/
Women's Lives (Fiction)

*"Noble is a supple storyteller who moves easily through time and among many points of view. Her characters are familiar and sympathetic, flaws and all. Barbara's smart, funny, sensible voice rescues this story from cliche and sentimentality."—**The Boston Globe***

"Noble's fourth novel (after Alphabet Weekends*) is a bittersweet yet ultimately uplifting story of love, family, and the bonds between mothers and daughters and among sisters. Letters and journal entries are sprinkled throughout the narrative, expanding the novel's focus to include the family's history from the very beginning and making for a sweeping, engaging, and comfortable women's fiction choice."—**Library Journal***

SUMMARY: How do you cope in a world without your mother? When Barbara realizes time is running out, she writes letters to her four daughters, aware that they'll be facing the trials and triumphs of life without her at their side. But how can she leave them when they still have so much growing up to do? Take Lisa, in her midthirties but incapable of making a commitment; or Jennifer, trapped in a stale marriage and buttoned up so tight she could burst. Twentysomething Amanda, the traveler, has always distanced herself from the rest of the family; and then there's Hannah, a teenage girl on the verge of womanhood. But by drawing on the wisdom in Barbara's letters, the girls might just find a way to cope with their loss.

ABOUT THE AUTHOR: **Elizabeth Noble** is the author of the internationally bestselling novels *The Reading Group, The Friendship Test,* and *Alphabet Weekends.* She lives with her husband and their two daughters in New York City.

1. What would you say in a letter to your daughter? What advice would you give?

2. How does the author succeed in portraying a main character who never actually appears in the novel?

3. Is it selfless or selfish for Barbara to reveal what she does?

4. What does each character learn about herself and what do they learn from Barbara?

5. How does each character handle grief?

6. What does it mean to have a "good death?"

7. How is each sister's relationship with her mother different?

8. Do you think it is important to keep a journal? Why or why not?

9. Is it ok to read another person's diary, letters, journal after they die? Why or why not? If you found someone's diary, would you read it?

10. What is the best advice your mother gave to you or what do you wish she'd told you?

11. Does birth order play a role in family dynamics and did the sister's here display characteristics that you'd expect from the eldest, middle, and youngest? Why or why not?

12. How do you think Barbara's daughters have been affected by their mother's romantic/marital history, and what role may her divorce have played in their own development and attitudes?

13. How do you view the author's portrayal of men within the narrative? In particular, how does Mark's reaction to his wife's death, in the context of his role as father and stepfather, affect you?

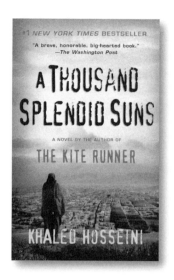

A THOUSAND SPLENDID SUNS

AUTHOR: *Khaled Hosseini*

PUBLISHER: Riverhead Books, 2008

WEBSITE: www.khaledhosseini.com
www.penguin.com

AVAILABLE IN:
Trade Paperback, 432 pages, $16.00
ISBN: 978-1-594-48385-1

SUBJECT: Culture & World Issues/
Family/Relationships (Fiction)

*"A fine risk-taking novel about two-victimized but courageous Afghan women. . . . Another artistic triumph, and surefire bestseller, for this fearless writer."—**Kirkus Reviews** (starred review)*

*"A brave, honorable, big-hearted book."—**The Washington Post***

From the #1 *New York Times* bestselling author of *The Kite Runner*

SUMMARY: Born a generation apart, and with very different ideas about love and family, Mariam and Laila are two women brought jarringly together by war, by loss and by fate. As they endure the ever escalating dangers around them—in their home as well as on the streets of Kabul—they come to form a bond that makes them both sisters and mother-daughter to each other, and that will ultimately alter the course not just of their own lives but of the next generation. With heart-wrenching power and suspense, Hosseini shows how a woman's love for her family can move her to shocking and heroic acts of self-sacrifice, and that in the end it is love, or even the memory of love, that is often the key to survival.

ABOUT THE AUTHOR: **Khaled Hosseini** was born in Kabul, Afghanistan, in 1965. In 2003, *The Kite Runner* was published and has since become an international bestseller, published in 48 countries. In 2006 he was named a goodwill envoy to UNHCR, the United Nations Refugee Agency. His second novel, *A Thousand Splendid Suns* was published in May of 2007. Currently, *A Thousand Splendid Suns* is published in 40 countries. Khaled has been working to provide humanitarian assistance in Afghanistan through The Khaled Hosseini Foundation. He lives in northern California.

1. The phrase "a thousand splendid suns," from the poem by Saib-e-Tabrizi, is quoted twice in the novel—once as Laila's family prepares to leave Kabul, and again when she decides to return there from Pakistan. It is also echoed in one of the final lines: "Miriam is in Laila's own heart, where she shines with the bursting radiance of a thousand suns." Discuss the thematic significance of this phrase.

2. Mariam's mother tells her: "Women like us. We endure. It's all we have." Discuss how this sentiment informs Mariam's life and how it relates to the larger themes of the novel.

3. At several points in the story, Mariam and Laila pass themselves off as mother and daughter. What is the symbolic importance of this subterfuge? In what ways is Mariam's and Laila's relationship with each other informed by their relationships with their own mothers?

4. One of the Taliban judges at Mariam's trial tells her, "God has made us different, you women and us men. Our brains are different. You are not able to think like we can. Western doctors and their science have proven this." What is the irony in this statement? How is irony employed throughout the novel?

5. The driver who takes Babi, Laila, and Tariq to the giant stone Buddhas above the Bamiyan Valley describes the crumbling fortress of Shahr-e-Zohak as "the story of our country, one invader after another . . . we're like those walls up there. Battered, and nothing pretty to look at, but still standing." Discuss the metaphorical import of this passage as it relates to Miriam and Laila. In what ways does their story reflect the larger story of Afghanistan's troubled history?

6. The film *Titanic* becomes a sensation on the black market. Why would people risk the Taliban's violent reprisals for a taste of popcorn entertainment? What do the Taliban's restrictions on such material say about the power of artistic expression and the threat it poses to repressive political regimes?

7. While the first three parts of the novel are written in the past tense, the final part is written in present tense. What do you think was the author's intent in making this shift? How does it change the effect of this final section?

A THREAD OF TRUTH

AUTHOR: *Marie Bostwick*

PUBLISHER: Kensington Books, 2009

WEBSITE: www.kensingtonbooks.com
www.mariebostwick.com

AVAILABLE IN:
Trade Paperback, 352 pages, $15.00
ISBN: 978-0-7582-3215-1

SUBJECT: Social Issues/Women's Lives/
Relationships (Fiction)

"Stitched into the heartwarming second installment of Bostwick's contemporary New England quilters series is an unbreakable thread of friendship and faith."—**Publishers Weekly**

"A pleasant story of friendship, with a message of starting over despite the odds. It will remind readers of Debbie Macomber . . . highly recommended."—**Library Journal**

SUMMARY: Come home to Marie Bostwick's poignant novel of new beginnings, old friends, and the rich, varied tapestry of lives fully lived. At twenty-seven, having fled an abusive marriage with little more than her kids and the clothes on her back, Ivy Peterman figures she has nowhere to go but up. Quaint, historic New Bern, Connecticut, seems as good a place as any to start fresh. With a part-time job at the Cobbled Court Quilt Shop and budding friendships, Ivy feels hopeful for the first time in ages. But when a popular quilting TV show is taped at the quilt shop, Ivy's unwitting appearance in an on-air promo alerts her ex-husband to her whereabouts. Suddenly, Ivy is facing the fight of her life—one that forces her to face her deepest fears as a woman and a mother. This time, however, she's got a sisterhood behind her: companions as complex, strong, and lasting as the quilts they stitch.

ABOUT THE AUTHOR: **Marie Bostwick** was born and raised in the Northwest. Since marrying the love of her life twenty-four years ago, she has never known a moment's boredom. Marie has three handsome sons and now lives with her husband in Connecticut where she writes, reads, quilts, and is active in her local church.

1. What is it about working with one's hands that cultivates a sense of serenity? Can you recall a time when quilting, knitting, or some other handiwork helped you through a tough time?

2. The specter of domestic violence forms the underpinning of Marie Bostwick's plot in *A Thread of Truth*. What moment in the story best captures the fear and helplessness Ivy feels about her situation? How else does Bostwick convey the reality of being a mother on the run from an abusive husband?

3. What would you do if you thought someone you knew was being abused by a significant other? To whom would you turn if it happened to you?

4. The most dangerous time for a woman being abused is when she tries to leave someone. Does that explain why Ivy is less than forthcoming with the details of her life? Does that justify lying to her boss? To her caseworker at the shelter? Where would someone in your community go if she was trying to escape from an abusive spouse?

5. In *A Thread of Truth*, Ivy presents herself to the shelter intake worker as "poor, powerless, and poorly educated," counting on the stereotype of victims of domestic violence to quell any doubts the woman might have about her. Yet studies show abuse happens in all kinds of families and relationships, and persons of any class, culture, religion, sexual orientation, age, and sex can be victims—or perpetrators—of domestic violence. Why do such stereotypes endure? What would it take to change them?

6. What do you think about Ivy's reluctance to come clean with her new friends about her past? Is her reluctance reasonable? Or does it contribute to her problems? Why are people so reluctant to share the less-than-perfect aspects of their lives with others? With whom do you share your unvarnished truth?

7. Many people hesitate to delve too deeply into the lives of those around them, yet the 2004 Allstate Foundation National Poll on Domestic Violence found three-out-of-four respondents personally knew a victim of domestic violence. And the American Psychological Association estimates 40% to 60% of men who abuse women also abuse children. Do these statistics make you more inclined to reach out to someone you suspect might be in an abusive relationship? Do you know the signs of abuse?

8. When it came to opening Cobbled Court Quilts, Ivy had the support of a wonderful circle of women—all pitched in to help in a way once seen only in families. How would you go about building such a foundation of friendship in your own life? Or have you already done so?

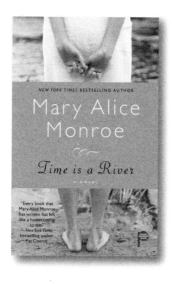

TIME IS A RIVER

AUTHOR: *Mary Alice Monroe*

PUBLISHER: Pocket Books, 2009

WEBSITE: www.simonandschuster.com

AVAILABLE IN:
Trade Paperback, 400 pages, $15.00
ISBN: 978-1-4165-4664-1

SUBJECT: Love & Romance/
Relationships/Personal Triumph (Fiction)

Mary Alice Monroe was awarded the 2008 Award for Writing from the South Carolina Center for the book. *Time Is a River* **was a** *USA Today* **"Summer 2008" pick for best summer books, an Indie Next Pick, and a** *Woman's Day* **"best beach read."**

SUMMARY: *Time Is a River* is an insightful novel that will sweep readers away to the seductive southern landscape, joining books by authors such as Anne Rivers Siddons and Sue Monk Kidd. Recovering from breast cancer and reeling from her husband's infidelity, Mia Landan flees her Charleston home to heal in the mountains near Asheville, North Carolina. She seeks refuge in a neglected fishing cabin belonging to her fly-fishing instructor, Belle Carson. Belle recently inherited the cabin from Kate Watkins, her grandmother she never knew. Little does Belle know that by opening the doors to Mia for a summer's sanctuary, she will open again the scandal that plagued Belle's family for generations.

A story timeless in its appeal emerges, with a power that reopens old wounds, but also brings a transforming healing for Mia, for Kate's descendants, and for all those in Mia's new community.

ABOUT THE AUTHOR: **Mary Alice Monroe** is *The New York Times* bestselling author of eleven novels, including *Time is a River, Sweetgrass, Skyward, The Beach House, The Four Seasons*, and *The Book Club*. She is an active conservationist and lives in the low-country of South Carolina.

1. What does the title, *Time is a River*, represent for you? What characteristics do the passing of time and the flowing of the river share? How did time and the river act as representations for one another in the story? Why did the river come to mean so much to Mia?

2. The road to healing does not follow a straight course. The opening of the book reflects a backwards and forward movement. Cite the small steps forward Mia takes and the subsequent set backs as she gradually gains strength and purpose. Discuss how the movement of casting—back and forth—symbolizes this pattern of healing.

3. Go back and read the Mark Nepo poem, "Holding Each Other Up" that opens the novel. What is the significance of opening the narrative with this poem?

4. By the end of the book, do you think Mia believes in fairy tales again? Discuss how the mountainous landscape and Mia's experiences in Watkin's Mill can be likened to a fairy tale?

5. Discuss Mia's relationship with her sister Maddie. How is Maddie like a mother to Mia; how is she like a sister? How like a friend? What is the difference?

6. At the start of the novel, Mia is in need of rescue and Belle is there for her. How do their roles reverse by the end of the summer? In your experience have you found that friendships are strengthened when each person gives and takes?

7. Do you think rain had any significance in Mia's story? Did you notice that important events seemed to happen during a downpour? Being that nature was so important to Mia, could this have been nature's way of acting as an actual character in the story?

8. In what ways does Belle's cabin have a soul and a spirit? Have you ever felt that a place or an object has a personality or a soul?

9. If you were to fill a hope chest today, with your most prized possessions, what would you include? What would these things say about you should somebody find them 50 years from now?

10. Are there any women in your life who have been so meaningful to you that they feel like family? Who has been like a sister to you? Who like a grandmother?

11. Discuss how Mia's journey to a remote cabin in the mountains reflects a fairy tale. Classic fairy tale structures are included in the novel. Find examples and discuss each: the old wise woman; the magical hut or sanctuary; feminine solidarity; dressing as a male; a caring lover; transformation; and a restored, renewed world order.

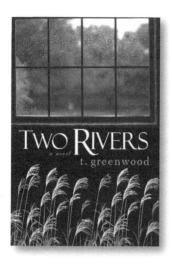

TWO RIVERS

AUTHOR: *T. Greenwood*

PUBLISHER: Kensington Books, 2009

WEBSITE: www.kensingtonbooks.com

AVAILABLE IN:
Trade Paperback, 352 pages, $15.00
ISBN: 978-0-7582-2877-2

SUBJECT: Family/Social Issues/
Relationships (Fiction)

*"Greenwood is a writer of subtle strength, evoking small-town life beautifully while spreading out the map of Harper's life, finding light in the darkest of stories."—**Publishers Weekly***

SUMMARY: T. Greenwood's new novel is a powerful, haunting tale of enduring love, destructive secrets, and opportunities that arrive in disguise.

In Two Rivers, Vermont, Harper Montgomery is living a life overshadowed by grief and guilt. Since the death of his wife, Betsy, twelve years earlier, Harper has narrowed his world to working at the local railroad and raising his daughter, Shelly, the best way he knows how. He wants only to make amends for his past mistakes.

Then one fall day, a train derails in Two Rivers, and amid the wreckage Harper finds an unexpected chance at atonement. One of the survivors, a pregnant fifteen-year-old girl with mismatched eyes and skin the color of blackberries, needs a place to stay. Though filled with misgivings, Harper offers to take Maggie in. But it isn't long before he begins to suspect that Maggie's appearance in Two Rivers is not the simple case of happenstance it first appeared to be.

ABOUT THE AUTHOR: **T. Greenwood** is the author of *Breathing Water, Nearer Than the Sky*, and *Undressing the Moon,* the latter two both Book Sense 76 picks. She teaches creative writing at The George Washington University in Washington, D.C., and at The Writer's Center in Bethesda, MD. She lives with her husband and their two daughters in the D.C. area.

1. At the beginning of the novel, Harper suggests that twelve years after the incident at the river he wants only to find forgiveness, to make amends for his involvement in the crime. Do you think that by the end of the novel he has done so? Why or why not? Is he forgiven? If so, by whom? Do you, the reader, forgive him?

2. Discuss the role that race plays in this novel. Is the crime against the carny racially motivated? Does what happened to Harper's mother factor into this decision? What are Brooder's motives?

3. What role does religion play in this novel? Do you think that Harper believes in God? Of what significance is the scene at the makeshift chapel in Roxbury?

4. *Two Rivers*, at its core, is a love story. Discuss the relationship between Harper and Betsy (both as children and as young adults). Does the tragedy of losing Betsy justify Harper's involvement in the scene at the river? Consider the blackberry imagery . . . both in the description of the carny's skin color and the memory he has of Betsy plucking a blackberry in summertime.

5. Discuss the mothers in this novel: Mrs. Parker, Helen Wilder, Betsy. How do each of them reject/redefine/embrace motherhood? Are they victims of their times? Why or why not?

6. What sacrifices do you think she makes to keep Harper from going to Vietnam? Did she have a choice? She blamed her father's stroke for trapping her in Two Rivers, so how do you think she feels after he died? Does she still feel trapped, now by her own pregnancy?

7. Could Harper and his new family have moved on without leaving? Where do you see his relationship with Brenda going, and do you think it could have gone there if they hadn't left Two Rivers?

8. What are some of the stronger images that stood out to you? How do they tie together Harper's past and present?

9. How did the civil rights movement and the Vietnam War change Harper's life and shape his views? Would you have made the same choices if you were in his situation at that time? Today?

10. All of the flashbacks to the fall of 1968 are in the third person point of view except for the last one, which is told through Harper's first person account. What is the significance of this change?

11. Discuss the symbolism of the two rivers and their confluence.

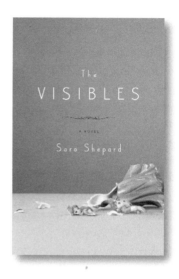

THE VISIBLES

AUTHOR: *Sara Shepard*

PUBLISHER: Free Press, 2009

WEBSITE: www.simonandschuster.com
www.sarashepard.com

AVAILABLE IN:
Hardcover, 336 pages, $24.00
ISBN: 978-1-416-5973-0

SUBJECT: Family/Identity/Coming of Age
(Fiction)

"Tightly constructed and captivating. . . . The Visibles is complicated, rewarding and full of heart. Shepard creates a rich reading experience in shying from simple answers and happy endings."—**Publishers Weekly**

"The big stuff is in here: coming of age; New York in the nineties; the complications of family and friendship; illness and ambition; hope and disappointment and redemption."—**Charles Bock, author of** *Beautiful Children*

SUMMARY: The only piece of information that Summer Davis takes away from her years at Peninsula Upper School—one of the finest in the Brooklyn Heights-to-Park Slope radius, to quote the promotional materials—is the concept that DNA defines who we are and forever ties us to our relatives. Or, does it? In a novel consumed by the uncertainties of science, the flaws of our parents, and enough loss and longing to line a highway, Sara Shepard is a penetrating chronicler of the adolescence we all carry into adulthood: how what happens to you as a kid never leaves you, how the fallibility of your parents can make you stronger, and how being right isn't as important as being wise. *The Visibles* investigates the secrets of the past, and the hidden corners of our own hearts, to find out whether real happiness is a gift or a choice.

ABOUT THE AUTHOR: **Sara Shepard** received an MFA in fiction writing from Brooklyn College and is the author of the young adult series *Pretty Little Liars*, a New York Public Library Notables selection. She lives in Philadelphia, Pennsylvania. This is her first adult novel.

1. When they are growing up, how are Summer and Claire similar and different? When they meet years later, how does Summer interpret the changes that each has gone through? Are they more alike later in life? What in Summer draws her to reconnect with Claire?

2. Periodically throughout the book, another voice enters the story. What effect did this have on your reading? When did you realize who the voice was and why it was important?

3. How does the author use the setting—time and place—to frame the story? What effect do the time lapses throughout the story have?

4. In the beginning of the novel, Summer's brother, Steven, barely reacts to their mother's disappearance. The next time we meet him, he is deeply and perhaps irrationally motivated by the first World Trade bombing. Then he is indifferent and unavailable, but by the end of the book, he has changed again. Has he adjusted better than Summer has by the novel's close? What drives his changes and behavior throughout the years?

5. What was the effect of reading the storyline through Summer's eyes? How would it have been different if her father had done all of the narrating? Or Stella?

6. In this story, and in life, how important are accidents, genetic and otherwise, to the shaping of a person?

7. Do you believe that Summer has faith? How does she express her faith? Does her faith change throughout the story?

8. Do you believe that Summer is not "equipped" to love during the course of the book? Why or why not? Is Summer capable of love by the end of the book? If so, what in her changed?

9. Throughout the story several characters—her mother, grandmother, and Stella—leave Summer's life. How does she react to each? How does each loss change the way that she thinks? How does it affect the people around her?

10. When did you discover Summer's father's secret? How did you react? Did you expect it? Do secrets have the capability to shape our lives more than truth? How and why?

11. Whose story is this? Is it Summer's story or is it her father's? Who changes the most from the beginning to the end?

Sara Shepard is available to speak by phone to reading groups. Please contact Jill Siegel—Jill.Siegel@simonandschuster.com.

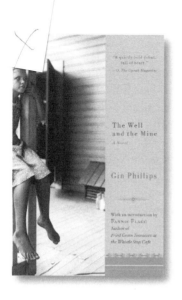

THE WELL AND THE MINE

AUTHOR: *Gin Phillips*

PUBLISHER: Riverhead Books, 2009

WEBSITE: www.penguin.com

AVAILABLE IN:
Trade Paperback, 304 pages, $15.00
ISBN: 978-1-59448-449-0

SUBJECT: Family/Relationships/
Personal Discovery (Fiction)

**Winner of the 2008 Barnes & Noble
Discover Great New Writers Fiction Award**

"A quietly bold debut, full of heart."—**O, The Oprah Magazine**

"Gin Phillips has a remarkable ear for dialogue and a tenderhearted eye for detail; you can hear the pecans and hickory nuts falling from the trees and feel the stillness of a hot summer night. A whisper runs through the novel—the ghosts of places and people and luscious peach pies."
—Los Angeles Times

SUMMARY: In a small Alabama coal-mining town during the summer of 1931, nine-year-old Tess Moore sits on her back porch and watches a woman toss a baby into her family's well without a word. This shocking act of violence sets in motion a chain of events that forces Tess and her older sister Virgie to look beyond their own door and learn the value of kindness and lending a helping hand. As Tess and Virgie try to solve the mystery of the well, an accident puts their seven-year-old brother's life in danger, forcing the Moore family to come to a new understanding of the power of love and compassion. A novel of warmth and true feeling, *The Well and the Mine* explores the value of community, charity, family, and hope we can give each other during a time of hardship

ABOUT THE AUTHOR: **Gin Phillips** is a freelance writer. A 1997 graduate of Birmingham-Southern College, she grew up in Montgomery, Alabama, and currently lives in Birmingham. *The Well and the Mine* is her first novel.

1. Virgie recollects, "Papa said it was an abomination what that woman did. That God would judge her." However, she refrains from judging and imagines the circumstances that might have driven the Well Woman to the deed. Where does Virgie's compassion stem from?

2. Why doesn't Sheriff Taylor inform the Moores that the baby was already dead as soon as he receives the inquest results?

3. If the woman and the baby had been black, do you feel that the investigation would have proceeded differently?

4. When Virgie and Tess check on Lola Lowe's new baby, Lola immediately knows why they are there, and their schoolmate Ellen is clearly embarrassed to have them see her home. Did their attempts to solve the mystery do more harm than good? How pure were their motives?

5. After the stock market crash, Jesse Bridgeman, the banker, kills himself. Why do you think a person who—even after losing most of his money—still had more than most of the townspeople would commit suicide?

6. "Beans and onion. Squash and tomato. It was the different tastes together, the ones that it didn't make no sense at all to stick on the same form, that your tongue really remembered." Are there any other examples in the novel when Phillips uses food as a metaphor? What do these metaphors tell us about the world she creates?

7. Would Tess and Jack have learned the lesson their father hoped to impart by taking them to pick cotton if they hadn't encountered and become friends with the Talbert children?

8. Why doesn't Albert sue the brick company after their truck driver hits Jack? Such a decision would be unfathomable today. What do you think has changed about our society? Is the change for better or worse?

9. What do you think about Jonah's explanation of why he won't have dinner at the Moores? Would you, like Albert, have capitulated? How did Jack's accident affect Albert's position?

10. Jonah and Albert feel they can never be real friends because of their race. Have you ever had to disavow or stifle a friendship because of external social pressures?

11. Albert chooses to protect his family over fully expressing his friendship for Jonah. Do you think he made the right choice? What other choices do the characters in the book make that can be read as both good and bad?

12. Did Virgie and Tess do the right thing in keeping the Well Woman's identity a secret? How might their lives have turned out differently if she hadn't chosen their well?

WESLEY THE OWL
The Remarkable Love Story
of an Owl and His Girl

AUTHOR: *Stacey O'Brien*

PUBLISHER: Free Press, 2009

WEBSITE: www.simonandschuster.com
www.wesleytheowl.com

AVAILABLE IN:
Trade Paperback, 256 pages, $15.00
ISBN: 978-1-4165-5177-5

SUBJECT: Environment & Nature/
Relationships/Personal Discovery (Memoir)

"Affectionate, quirky, joyous, and wise, Wesley shows us the Way of the Owl—the way to God and grace. This book is destined to become a classic, and will deepen importantly the way we understand birds."
—Sy Montgomery, author of *The Good Good Pig*

SUMMARY: On Valentine's Day 1985, biologist Stacey O'Brien first met a four-day-old baby barn owl—a fateful encounter that would turn into an astonishing 19-year saga. With nerve damage in one wing, the owlet's ability to fly was forever compromised, and he had no hope of surviving on his own in the wild. O'Brien, a young assistant in the owl laboratory at Caltech, was immediately smitten, promising to care for the helpless owlet and give him a permanent home. *Wesley the Owl* is the funny, poignant story of their dramatic two decades together.

Enhanced by wonderful photos, *Wesley the Owl* is a thoroughly engaging, heartwarming, often funny story of a complex, emotional, non-human being capable of reason, play, and, most important, love and loyalty. It is sure to be cherished by animal lovers everywhere.

ABOUT THE AUTHOR: **Stacey O'Brien** is trained as a biologist specializing in wild-animal behavior. She graduated from Occidental College with a BS in biology and continued her education at Caltech. Stacey now works as a wildlife rescuer and rehabilitation expert with a variety of local animals, including the endangered brown pelican, owls, seabirds, possums, and songbirds. She lives in Southern California.

1. Do you think you could have done what the author did, devoting a good part of 19 years of her life to caring for an animal? Have you ever had a pet who demanded as much time, money, attention, and love as Wesley did? Did the way the pet and you relate to each other change as you both got older? Did your relationship with your pet change how you viewed the world?

2. How did Wesley help Stacey in her own life after she saved his? How did he save her life? What did she learn from Wesley that no other animal could have taught her?

3. What part of the book did you think was the funniest and what part did you think was the grossest? The biologists at the lab where Stacey works are very comfortable with animals. How do the relationships between scientists and the animals play a role in their scientific research and discoveries?

4. Think about the ways in which Stacey and Wesley were able to communicate with each other. To what extent do you think they understood one another? How is this similar to and different from communication between people? Communication between people and their pets? What are the differences between relating to an animal that lives a solitary life and relating to an animal that is predisposed to live in a social group or pack? What are the differences between relating to an animal that is wild and an animal that is domesticated?

5. What scientific discoveries did Stacey make about barn owls, and what surprised you most about barn owls? Before you read this book, what was your impression of barn owls? Did reading this book change your mind, and if so, in what ways?

Stacey O'Brien is available to speak by phone to reading groups. Please contact Andy Dodds—Andrew.dodds@simonandschuster.com

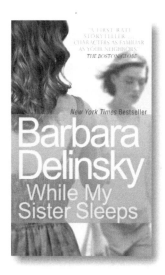

WHILE MY SISTER SLEEPS

AUTHOR: *Barbara Delinsky*

PUBLISHER: Anchor Books, 2009

WEBSITE: www.ReadingGroupCenter.com
www.barbaradelinsky.com

AVAILABLE IN:
Trade Paperback, 336 pages, $14.95
ISBN: 978-0-767-92895-3

SUBJECT: Family/Relationships/
Personal Challenges (Fiction)

"Delinsky is a first-rate storyteller who creates believable, sympathetic characters who seem as familiar as your neighbors."—**The Boston Globe**

"Delinsky is an engaging writer who knows how to interweave several stories about complex relationships and keeps her books interesting to the end."—**Newark Star-Ledger**

"Delinsky treads the same domestic themes as fellow best-seller Jodi Picoult."—**Entertainment Weekly**

SUMMARY: Once again *The New York Times* bestselling author Barbara Delinsky brings us a masterful family portrait, filled with thought-provoking insights into how emotions affect the decisions we make and how letting go can be the hardest thing to do and the greatest expression of love all at the same time.

Molly and Robin Snow are sisters in the prime of life. So when Molly receives the news that Robin has suffered a massive heart attack, the news couldn't be more shocking. At the hospital, the Snow family receives a grim prognosis: Robin may never regain consciousness. Feelings of guilt and jealousy flare up as Robin's family struggles to cope. It's up to Molly to make the tough decisions, and she soon makes discoveries that shatter some of her most cherished beliefs about the sister she thought she knew.

ABOUT THE AUTHOR: **Barbara Delinsky** is the author of more than seventeen bestselling novels with over twenty million copies in print. She has been published in twenty-five languages worldwide. Barbara lives with her family in New England.

1. How would you characterize the relationship among Robin, Molly, and Chris? Does Chris play a different role because he is a son? How does the Snow family compare to yours?

2. How is Molly transformed during the week after Robin's heart attack? What does Molly discover about herself and about the range of emotions she and her sister evoked in each other?

3. What is at the root of Kathryn's controlling behavior? How did her past, including her experience with her own parents and her art teacher, influence her personality? Who has more power in the marriage: Kathryn or Charlie?

4. Discuss Snow Hill and what it means to Molly's family. What makes the Snows good at nurturing plants but not as good at nurturing one another? What kinds of healing does Molly experience through her work at Snow Hill?

5. What do Charlie's religious beliefs say about him and about the differences between him and the other members of his family?

6. As parents, what family memories do Chris and Erin create for their daughter, Chloe? How does their approach to parenting compare to Charlie and Kathryn's?

7. How does Alexis's illness shape the novel's storyline? What parallels exist between her situation and Kathryn's state of denial?

8. How much is Nick entitled to know, as a reporter and as a friend of Robin's? Is Robin entitled to less privacy because she is a public figure, with a wide circle of fans who are concerned about her?

9. What determines whether Liz will be a threat to Chris's marriage? How is Liz's role in the novel different from Peter's? How much does the past matter in a marriage, especially events that took place before the wedding?

10. What was it like to read Robin's journal after hearing so much about her? Captured in her own words, how does her life compare to other people's impressions of her?

THE WHITE TIGER

AUTHOR: *Aravind Adiga*

PUBLISHER: Free Press, 2008

WEBSITE: www.simonandschuster.com
www.aravindadiga.com

AVAILABLE IN:
Trade Paperback, 304 pages, $14.00
ISBN: 978-1-4165-6260-3

SUBJECT: Culture & World Issues/
Relationships/Social Issues (Fiction)

"Compelling, angry, and darkly humorous, The White Tiger *is an unexpected journey into a new India. Aravind Adiga is a talent to watch."*
—**Mohsin Hamid, author of** *The Reluctant Fundamentalist*

"Darkly comic. . . . Balram's appealingly sardonic voice and acute observations of the social order are both winning and unsettling."—***The New Yorker***

SUMMARY: Balram Halwai is a complicated man. Servant. Philosopher. Entrepreneur. Murderer. Over the course of seven nights, by the scattered light of a preposterous chandelier, Balram tells us the terrible and transfixing story of how he came to be a success in life—having nothing but his own wits to help him along. Born in the dark heart of India, Balram gets a break when he is hired as a driver for his village's wealthiest man, two house Pomeranians (Puddles and Cuddles), and the rich man's (very unlucky) son. And with a charisma as undeniable as it is unexpected, Balram teaches us that religion doesn't create virtue, and money doesn't solve every problem—but decency can still be found in a corrupt world. Sold in sixteen countries around the world, *The White Tiger* recalls *The Death of Vishnu* and *Bangkok 8* in ambition, scope, and narrative genius, with a mischief and personality all its own. Amoral, irreverent, deeply endearing, and utterly contemporary, this novel is an international publishing sensation—and a startling, provocative debut.

ABOUT THE AUTHOR: **Aravind Adiga** was born in India in 1974 and attended Columbia and Oxford universities. A former correspondent for *Time* magazine, he has also been published in the *Financial Times*. He lives in Mumbai, India.

1. The author chose to tell the story from the provocative point of view of an exceedingly charming, egotistical admitted murderer. Do Balram's ambition and charisma make his vision clearer? Did he win you over?

2. Why does Balram choose to address the Premier? What motivates him to tell his story? What similarities does he see between himself and the Premier?

3. Because of his lack of education, Ashok calls Balram "half-baked." What does he mean by this? How does Balram go about educating himself? What does he learn?

4. Balram variously describes himself as "a man of action and change," "a thinking man," "an entrepreneur," "a man who sees tomorrow," and a "murderer." Is any one of these labels the most fitting, or is he too complex for only one? How would you describe him?

5. Balram blames the culture of servitude in India for the stark contrasts between the Light and the Darkness and the antiquated mind set that slows change. Discuss his rooster coop analogy and the role of religion, the political system, and family life in perpetuating this culture. What do you make of the couplet Balram repeats to himself: "I was looking for the key for years/but the door was always open"?

6. Discuss Balram's opinion of his master and how it and their relationship evolve. Balram says "where my genuine concern for him ended and where my self-interest began, I could not tell" (160). Where do you think his self-interest begins?

7. Compare Ashok and his family's actions after Pinky Madam hits a child to Balram's response when his driver does. Were you surprised at the actions of either?

8. Discuss Balram's reasons for the murder: fulfilling his father's wish that his son "live like a man," taking back what Ashok had stolen from him, and breaking out of the rooster coop, among them. Which ring true to you and which do not? Did you feel Balram was justified in killing Ashok? Discuss the paradox inherent in the fact that in order to live fully as a man, Balram took a man's life.

9. Balram's thoughts of his family initially hold him back from killing Ashok. What changes his mind? Why do you think he goes back to retrieve Dharam at the end of the novel? Does his decision absolve him in any way?

10. The novel offers a window into the rapidly changing economic situation in India. What do we learn about entrepreneurship and Balram's definition of it?

11. Do you think of the novel, ultimately, as a cautionary or hopeful tale?

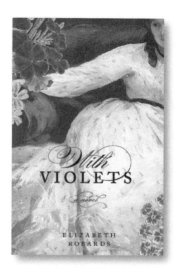

WITH VIOLETS

AUTHOR: *Elizabeth Robards*

PUBLISHER: Avon A, 2008

WEBSITE: www.avonbooks.com
www.elizabethrobards.typepad.com

AVAILABLE IN:
Trade Paperback, 320 pages, $13.95
ISBN: 978-0-061-57912-7

SUBJECT: Art/History/Women's Lives
(Historical Fiction)

"With deft brush strokes, Elizabeth Robards creates a wonderfully vivid portrait of the Second Empire and the dawn of Impressionism."—**Tracy Grant, author of** *Beneath a Silent Moon*

SUMMARY: Paris in the 1860s: a magnificent time of expression, where brilliant young artists rebel against the stodginess of the past to freely explore new styles of creating—and bold new ways of living. Passionate, beautiful, and utterly devoted to her art, Berthe Morisot is determined to be recognized as an important painter. But as a woman, she finds herself sometimes overlooked in favor of her male counterparts—Monet, Pissarro, Degas. And there is one great artist among them who captivates young Berthe like none other: the celebrated genius Édouard Manet, his life is a wildly overgrown garden of scandal. He becomes Berthe's mentor, her teacher . . . her lover, despite his curiously devoted marriage to his frumpy, unappealing wife, Suzanne. For a headstrong young woman from a respectable family, an affair with such an intoxicating scoundrel can only spell heartbreak and ruin. But Berthe refuses to resign herself to the life of quiet submission that Society has dictated for her. Undiscouraged, she will create her own destiny . . . and confront life—and love—on her own terms.

ABOUT THE AUTHOR: Award-winning author **Elizabeth Robards** formerly lived in France and has studied art and writing. Elizabeth has found Nirvana doing what she loves most—writing contemporary and historical women's fiction.

1. Did Édouard really love Berthe?
2. What were Édouard's feelings for Suzanne? She seemed so opposite of everything Édouard stood for, why do you suppose he married her?
3. If Édouard hadn't been married to Suzanne when he met Berthe, how do you think their relationship would have been different—or would it have changed anything?
4. Why do you think Édouard worked so hard to win Berthe back when she pulled away, yet when he could have her he didn't want her?
5. What would have happened if Berthe had gone away with Édouard when he asked her to drop everything and leave? Do you think he asked her to go away with him because he knew that ultimately she wouldn't be able to leave Paris and her family, or do you believe he was sincere?
6. Discuss the role of the upper class nineteenth century woman—compare and contrast Berthe with a more conventional lady of the day.
7. Impressionism was considered an avant-garde art form and the artists associated with it were considered radical and somewhat deviant in the way they bucked the system, essentially thumbing their noses at the conventional art celebrated by the Salon—compare and contrast this to the way Berthe lived her life.
8. By the heyday of Impressionism in the 1870s, the old city had been leveled and replaced by Baron Housemann's "City of Light," which is much like the Paris we know today: wide, lighted boulevards and elegant buildings. During this period of shift, nearly half a million working class people were displaced and forced to the Paris outskirts, while the affluent moved in to the beautiful, clean, new city. Compare and contrast this rebirth of Paris to the birth of Impressionism.
9. Do you think Berthe loved Édouard the man or was she in love with the illusion of Édouard the Rebel? Bring this thought into the 21st century, what role does hero worship play in our own lives?
10. Discuss the difference in how Americans and the French view adultery. Did Berthe simply become an "inconvenient mistress" to Édouard in the end?
11. Can you name instances of places in the story where the writing made you "see" her paintings?
12. Out of the circle of Impressionists, who would you most want to invite to a dinner party and why?
13. Do you believe a man and a woman can have an "intimate" but platonic friendship?

BE FOREWARNED:

These fourteen tales of transgressive
pleasure are guaranteed to arouse
your moral imagination.

**The Seven Deadly
Sins Sampler** includes
renowned authors such
as Flannery O'Connor,
Raymond Carver, and
William Faulkner, as well as
contemporaries like Tobias
Wolff and Perri Klass.

Available in the fall, **Even Deadlier**, the sequel
to the *Seven Deadly Sins Sampler*, ups the ante
with fourteen more stories from Jim Shepard,
Rose Tremain, Nadine Gordimer, Honoré de
Balzac, F. Scott Fitzgerald, and others.

Praise for *The Seven Deadly Sins Sampler*:

"It is instructive to hear what some of our greatest literary
lights have thought about good and evil, right and wrong, sin
and valor. If there are indeed seven deadly sins, this collection
will make you think differently about them and about yourself."

– Cathleen Falsani,
religion editor for the Chicago Sun-Times
and author of The God Factor

FOR MORE INFORMATION AND TO ORDER:
7DEADLIES.COM OR 800.222.5870

Looking for the next great book for your book club? LOOK NO FURTHER.

What if you had to steal something to save it?

The extraordinary #1 *New York Times* bestseller from Markus Zusak!

"BRILLIANT and hugely ambitious. . . . It's the kind of book that can be LIFE CHANGING."
—*The New York Times*

THE BOOK THIEF

MARKUS ZUSAK

THE EXTRAORDINARY *NEW YORK TIMES* #1 BESTSELLER

"Brilliant."
—*The New York Times Book Review*

"Poised to become a classic."
—*USA Today*

"A major achievement."
—*People* Magazine

"An absorbing and searing narrative."
—*The Washington Post Book-World*

"Intricate and extraordinary."
—*Newsday*

For discussion questions and more, visit **MarkusZusak.com**

Available wherever books are sold.

ALFRED A. KNOPF

extremely witty conversation with southern authors
most excellent recommendations for reading
clever & refined musings of booksellers & writers
engaging & amusing author readings
illuminating excerpts from great southern books
and other such items as are of interest to
her ladyship, the editor

Lady Banks' Commonplace Book

front porch literary gossip
from your favorite southern bookshops

subscribe at ladybankscommonplacebook.com

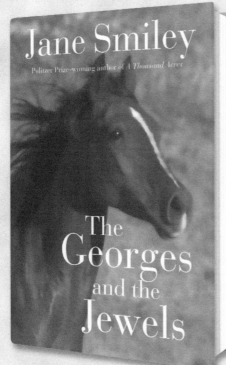

READING GROUP Choices

We wish to thank the authors, agents, publicists, librarians, booksellers, and our publishing colleagues who have continued to support this publication by calling to our attention some quality books for group discussion, and the publishers and friends who have helped to underwrite this edition.

Alfred A. Knopf

Algonquin Books

Anchor Books

Atlantic Monthly Press

Avon A

Berkley Books

Da Capo Press

Dial Press

Downtown Press

Free Press

Fulcrum Publishing

Great Books Foundation

Harper paperbacks

Harper Perennial

Hyperion

Kensington Books

Mariner Books

Middleway Press

New American Library

Penguin Books

Picador USA

Plume Books

Pocket Books

Random House Children's Books

Riverhead Books

Southern Independent Booksellers Alliance

Unbridled Books

Vanguard Press

Vintage Books

Reading Group Choices' goal is to join with publishers, bookstores, libraries, trade associations, and authors to develop resources to enhance the reading group experience.

Reading Group Choices is distributed annually to bookstores, libraries, and directly to book groups. Titles from previous issues are posted on the **www.ReadingGroupChoices.com** website. Books presented here have been recommended by book group members, librarians, booksellers, literary agents, publicists, authors, and publishers. All submissions are then reviewed to ensure the discussibility of each title. Once a title is approved for inclusion by the Advisory Board (see below), publishers are asked to underwrite production costs, so that copies of *Reading Group Choices* can be distributed for a minimal charge.

For additional copies, please call your local library or bookstore, or contact us by phone or email as shown below. Quantities are limited. For more information, please visit our website at **www.ReadingGroupChoices.com**

Toll-free: 1-866-643-6883 • info@ReadingGroupChoices.com

READING GROUP CHOICES' ADVISORY BOARD

Donna Paz Kaufman founded the bookstore training and consulting group of Paz & Associates in 1992, with the objective of creating products and services to help independent bookstores and public libraries remain viable in today's market. A few years later, she met and married **Mark Kaufman**, whose background included project management, marketing communications, and human resources. Together, they launched **Reading Group Choices** in 1994 to bring publishers, booksellers, libraries, and readers closer together. They sold **Reading Group Choices** to Barbara and Charlie Mead in May 2005. They now offer training and education for new and prospective booksellers, architectural design services for bookstores and libraries, marketing support, and a training library for professional and staff development on a wide variety of topics. To learn more about Paz & Associates, visit www.PazBookBiz.com.

John Mutter is editor-in-chief of *Shelf Awareness*, the daily e-mail newsletter focusing on books, media about books, retailing and related issues to help booksellers, librarians and others do their jobs more effectively.

Before he and his business partner, Jenn Risko, founded the company in May 2005, he was executive editor of bookselling at *Publishers Weekly*. He has covered book industry issues for 25 years and written for a variety of publications, including *The Bookseller* in the U.K.; *Australian Bookseller & Publisher*; *Boersenblatt*, the German book trade magazine; and *College Store Magazine* in the U.S. For more information about *Shelf Awareness*, go to its Web site, www.shelf-awareness.com.

Mark Nichols was an independent bookseller in various locations from Maine to Connecticut from 1976 through 1993. After seven years in a variety of positions with major publishers in New York and San Francisco, he joined the American Booksellers Association in 2000, and currently serves as Senior Director, Publisher Initiatives. He is on the Board of James Patterson's ReadKiddoRead.com, and has edited two volumes with Newmarket Press—*Book Sense Best Books* (2004) and *Book Sense Best Children's Books* (2005).

Nancy Olson has owned and operated Quail Ridge Books & Music in Raleigh, NC, since 1984, which has grown from 1,200 sq. ft. to 9,000+ sq. ft and sales of $3.2 million. The bookstore won three major awards in 2001: *Publishers Weekly* Bookseller of the Year, Charles Haslam Award for Excellence in Bookselling; Pannell Award for Excellence in Children's Bookselling. It was voted "Best in the Triangle" in the *Independent Weekly* and *Metro Magazine*.

Jill A. Tardiff is publishing industry consultant and project manager working under her banner company Bamboo River Associates. She is also advertising manager for such print and online publications as *Parabola—Tradition, Myth, and the Search for Meaning*, as well as contributing editor at *Publishers Weekly*. Jill is the past president of the Women's National Book Association (WNBA) and WNBA-New York City chapter, 2004–2006 and 2000–2005, respectively. She is currently WNBA's National Reading Group Month Committee Chair and Coordinator and its United Nations Department of Public Information NGO Chief Representative. She is currently working on several book proposals on modern-day pilgrimage.

Book Group Resources

WEBSITES

About reading groups and book clubs

- **ReadingGroupChoices.com**—Over 1000 guides available plus giveaways and fun and interactive materials for reading groups.

- **bookgroupexpo.com**—Come to book group expo and celebrate.

- **Book-Clubs-Resource.com**—A guide to book clubs and reading groups with a collection of links and information for readers, including information about saving with discount book clubs.

- **BookClubCookbook.com**—Recipes and food for thought from your book club's favorite books and authors

- **bookclubgirl.com**—Dedicated to sharing great books, news, and tips with book club girls everywhere

- **bookgroupbuzz.booklistonline.com**—Book group tips, reading lists, & lively talk of literary news from the experts at Booklist Online

- **NationalReadingGroupMonth.org**—Celebrating the joy of shared reading

- **Literaryaffairs.com**—Live a life a passion inspired by literature

About Books

- **ShelfAwareness.com**—A free e-mail newsletter dedicated to helping the people in stores, in libraries and on the Web buy, sell, and lend books most wisely.

- **GenerousBooks.com**—A community for those who love books and love to discuss them

- **BookMuse.com**— Commentary, author bios, and suggestions for further reading

- **BookBrowse.com**— Book reviews, excerpts, and author interviews

- **BookSpot.com**—Help in your search for the best book-related content on the Web

- **Publisher Web Sites**—Find additional topics for discussion, special offers for book groups, and other titles of interest.

Alfred A. Knopf – **randomhouse.com**

Algonguin Books — **algonquin.com**

Anchor Books — **readinggroupcenter.com**

Atlantic Monthly Press — **groveatlantic.com**

Avon A — **avonbooks.com**

Berkley Books — **penguin.com**

Da Capo Lifelong Books — **dacapopress.com**

Dial Press Trade Paperbacks — **randomhouse.com**

Downtown Press — **simonandschuster.com**

Free Press — **simonandschuster.com**

Fulcrum Publishing — **fulcrum-books.com**

Harper paperbacks — **harpercollins.com**

Harper Perennial — **harperperennial.com**

Hyperion Books — **hyperionbooks.com**

Kensington Books — **kensingtonbooks.com**

Mariner Books — **hmhbooks.com**

Middleway Press — **middlewaypress.com**

New American Library — **penguin.com**

Penguin Books — **penguin.com**

Picador USA — **us.macmillan.com**

Plume Books — **penguin.com**

Pocket Books — **simonandschuster.com**

Random House Children's Books — **randomhouse.com**

Riverhead Books — **penguin.com**

Unbridled Books — **unbridledbooks.com**

Vanguard Press — **vanguardpressbooks.com**

Vintage Books — **readinggroupcenter.com**

BOOKS

Between the Covers: The Book Babes' Guide to a Woman's Reading Pleasures by Margo Hammond and Ellen Heltzel. De Capo Press, ISBN 978-0-7382-1229-6 $16.95

The Book Club Companion: A Comprehensive Guide to the Reading Group Experience by Diana Loevy. Berkeley Books, ISBN 0-425-21009-X, $14.00.

The Book Club Cookbook: Recipes and Food for Thought from Your Book Club's Favorite Books and Authors by Judy Gelman and Vicki Levy Krupp. Tarcher/Penguin, ISBN 1-58542-322-X, $15.95.

The Book Group Book: A Thoughtful Guide to Forming and Enjoying a Stimulating Book Discussion Group. Edited by Ellen Slezak and Margaret Eleanor Atwood. Chicago Review Press, ISBN 1-5565-2412-9, $14.95.

Book Lust: Recommended Reading for Every Mood, Moment, and Reason by Nancy Pearl. Sasquatch Books, ISBN 1-57061-381-8, $16.95.

More Book Lust: Recommended Reading for Every Mood, Moment, and Reason by Nancy Pearl. Sasquatch Books, ISBN 1-57061-435-0 $16.95.

Book Smart: Your Essential Reading List for Becoming a Literary Genius in 365 Days by Jane Mallison. McGraw Hill, ISBN 978-0-07-148271-4, $14.95

Family Book Sharing Groups: Start One in Your Neighborhood! by Marjorie R. Simic with Eleanor C. MacFarlane. The Family Literacy Center, ISBN 1-8837-9011-5, $6.95.

Good Books Lately: The One-Stop Resource for Book Groups and Other Greedy Readers by Ellen Moore and Kira Stevens. St. Martin's Griffin, ISBN 978-0-312-30961-9, $13.95.

Leave Me Alone, I'm Reading: Finding and Losing Myself in Books by Maureen Corrigan. Random House, ISBN 0-375-50425-7, $24.95.

The Mother-Daughter Book Club: How Ten Busy Mothers and Daughters Came Together to Talk, Laugh and Learn Through Their Love of Reading by Shireen Dodson and Teresa Barker. HarperCollins, ISBN 0-0609-5242-3, $14.

Running Book Discussion Groups by Lauren Zina John. Neal-Schuman, ISBN 1-55570-542-1.

The Reading Group Handbook: Everything You Need to Know to Start Your Own Book Club by Rachel Jacobsohn. Hyperion, ISBN 0-786-88324-3, $12.95.

Recipe for a Book Club: A Monthly Guide for Hosting Your Own Reading Group: Menus & Recipes, Featured Authors, Suggested Readings, and Topical Questions by Mary O'Hare and Rose Storey. Capital Books, ISBN 978-1-931-86883-9, $19.95.

Women's Fiction Authors: A Research Guide by Rebecca Vnuk. Libraries Unlimited, ISBN 978-1-591-58642-5, $40.00.

Talking About Books: Literature Discussion Groups in K–8 Classrooms by Kathy Short. Heinemann, ISBN 0-3250-0073-5, $24.

Thirteen Ways of Looking at the Novel by Jane Smiley. Knopf, ISBN 1-4000-4059-0, $26.95.

What to Read: The Essential Guide for Reading Group Members and Other Book Lovers (Revised) by Mickey Pearlman. HarperCollins, ISBN 0-0609-5313-6, $14.00.

A Year of Reading: A Month-By-Month Guide to Classics and Crowd-Pleasers for You or Your Book Group by H. E. Ellington and Jane Freimiller. Sourcebooks, ISBN 1-5707-1935-7, $14.95.

Two Great Features
on **ReadingGroupChoices.com**

MUSIC BY THE BOOK!
A pairing of music and words just for book groups!

In **MUSIC BY THE BOOK!**, Tom Moon, author of *1,000 Recordings to Hear Before You Die*, chooses different music selections that accompany book group picks.

Award-winning music journalist Tom Moon has searched out peak musical experiences from all genres and every corner of the earth. *1000 Recordings To Hear Before You Die* is the result of his journey. Covering both acknowledged world-culture masterworks and recordings that have been unfairly overlooked, the book is designed to encourage listeners to become explorers. Tom has also developed a Listening Group Guide to enhance the music lover's listening experience! Please contact Michael Rockliff to receive the Guide (mrockliff@workman.com) and visit www.1000recordings.com for more information about the joy of music.

For your next gathering, why not pair a book selection from *Reading Group Choices* with a music choice from **MUSIC BY THE BOOK!**

WINE BY THE BOOK!
A pairing of music and words just for book groups!

In **WINE BY THE BOOK!**, Laurie Forster, The Wine Coach® and author of *The Sipping Point: A Crash Course in Wine*, explores wines from regions found in book group picks.

In *The Sipping Point: A Crash Course in Wine*, Laurie gives general tips on wine essentials, including how to order wine at dinner, simplify food pairings, handle awkward wine moments, and even bounce back the morning after! Laurie's first book reflects her fresh perspective on wine education and has already received rave reviews. *The Sipping Point* won a Living Now Book Award for Cooking/Entertaining books. Please visit www.thewinecoach.com for more information about the joy of wine.

For your next gathering, why not pair a book selection from *Reading Group Choices* with a wine choice from **WINE BY THE BOOK!**

Two more discussible ideas to check out on
ReadingGroupChoices.com!

INDEX BY SUBJECT/INTEREST